Exposure Ni

10   ᴐ Get
More stomers
from the Internet in
2014

Fast, Effective and Future Proof Online
Marketing Strategies for Businesses

Tim Kitchen, Amen Sharma, Kavita Prashar, Mike De La
Victoria & Kevin Famador

Free lifetime updates and Online Marketing Review
worth £186 at
www.ExposureNinja.com/101

Introduction

The world of Internet Marketing changes fast and in 2014 the landscape looks very different to how it did a couple of years ago. The good news is that whatever your business, more of your customers are online than ever before. And their familiarity with the Internet means an increase in purchases, contacts and bookings made over the web.

But this opportunity also brings complexity. More competition, mobile traffic, advertising innovations, social media… there's as much to get wrong as there is to get right.

We spend all day every day analysing, planning and doing online marketing for businesses across the world in every possible industry. We live this stuff 10-12 hours a day, 6 days per week in the trenches. Our books on SEO and social media help thousands of businesses get to grips with their online marketing, and hearing their success stories is incredibly gratifying.

This book is here to help you make the most of the Internet in 2014 and take your business to the next level by attracting more customers, leads, contacts or whatever online success looks like for you. You'll read case studies, best practice tips and plenty of recommendations guided by our extensive experience in every element of online marketing.

How to Use this Book

The tips in this book are those we've found to be the most effective at generating more business. Some are short, some are longer. Some are small tweaks while some almost an entirely new marketing strategy. Some will help you attract new customers while others will help you to make more money from your *existing* customers.

We've grouped them into different categories to make it easier to navigate through so many strategies.

As the great Dan Kennedy says, marketing really boils down to a mixture of basic maths and behavioural psychology. Understanding *how* and *why* people buy, and shaping your business and marketing around this understanding, is the key to growth.

Just like getting your driving license gives you freedom, learning how to sell stuff to people means you'll never be poor. This book is the distillation of our experience doing exactly that for our clients and through our own businesses. The core principles of 'selling stuff to people' run through every tip.

How you consume and apply these tips is up to you. Whether you read through all the tips in one or two sittings or you dip in and out, you'll pick up some things that you'll want to apply immediately and others that you can put on your marketing to-do list.

And remember that knowledge isn't power. Knowledge is only *potential* power; it's the <u>application</u> of these strategies that will really make a difference to your business.

So dive in, dig around, enjoy and start experimenting.

Grammer and Speling

While we are effective online marketers, we are not professional authors. Hopefully this is the right way round, and the value you and your business gets from this book is through the tips themselves rather than the spelling and grammar which, although thoroughly checked, is bound to contain the odd error. We write how we speak and while that might make this book easy to read, it probably won't win us any literary prizes. We hope you enjoy the book and find it useful all the same.

Free Gifts worth £186 ($305) for Readers

As a thank you for purchasing this book and to give you a head start with your Ninja-style online marketing, we'd like to offer you two very special free gifts:

Gift 1:

Claim your FREE 7 Point Online Marketing Review from our world-class experts. Our review team will take a detailed look at your online marketing, your competitors and the potential in your market. They'll put together a customised strategic plan for you to attract more business from your website worth £186 +VAT. It's free and there's no catch. Head to http://exposureninja.com/101 to claim now.

Gift 2:

The strategies in this book are as future-proof as Internet strategies can be. However we'll be updating this book as technologies change, and things evolve. Rather than having to buy up-to-date versions, we want to give you lifetime updates, free of charge and again - no catch. Head to the same page (http://exposureninja.com/101) to sign up.

Technical Skill Requirements

You might be wondering what sort of technical skill you're going to need in order to implement the tips in this book. Most of the tips are easy enough to execute with very minimal technical skill. While it's certainly true that some of the tips will require changes to a website, setting up an email autoresponder or posting on social media, the technical bits cannot be allowed to get in the way of growing your business. If you can't implement the changes yourself, there is plenty of cheap help available to do it for you.

To include only the tips that required no technical skill would be to leave out some of the important ones. In cases where we had to decide whether or not to include a more advanced tip, we've decided to include it.

DIY vs Getting Help

The most important thing is that you understand *what* each strategy or technique is, and *why* you are adopting it, not necessarily *how* to execute it.

Not only is it irrelevant whether or not the CEO of Toyota can actually *build* a car, it would be inefficient use of his time to *learn* how to do so. But it'd be absolutely catastrophic if he decided to spend his time on the production line actually *building cars* instead of spending his time doing the important strategic things that only he can do. This sounds so obvious and yet we find business owners on a daily basis spending hours carrying out the most menial tasks in order to save themselves a few dollars, pounds or euros paying somebody who could do it to a higher standard in a fraction of the time.

When you decide to add a strategy to your marketing mix, first commit to seeing it through. If it's simple enough to carry it out yourself and you want to do it, plan to do so. If it's outside your technical competence, immediately act to have it carried out for you by a specialist. But do not let something that could have a significant impact on your business slip away just because you are unable to implement it yourself.

Online Marketing

We start our tips with some general online marketing principles. These are important because they form the basis of everything that comes afterwards. If Pay Per Click, SEO, Websites and Social Media are the pillars holding up the house, this first section is the solid foundation that everything else is built upon.

Know your positioning backwards

It's very rare in the offline world that customers to a particular type of shop will be faced with a row of dozens of such shops. A bride shopping for a wedding dress doesn't go to 'Wedding Dress Avenue' and get to choose between up to 20 different wedding dress shops.

Yet this is exactly what happens online. In all likelihood your customers are faced with a variety of businesses to choose from. Being just another face in the crowd is not a good strategic choice.

What we'd find if wedding dress avenue *were* to exist is that the shops who found their own niche and communicated this most effectively would be those who won. Exactly the same is true online. When faced with such a bewildering amount of choice, searchers tend to resort to price shopping when all else is perceived to be equal. The job of good positioning is not to allow all else to be as equal.

By clearly specifying exactly what makes you different, what sort of audience you're targeting and why this audience should buy from you, you increase the affinity they feel for your website and business, and increase the response rate amongst this type of customer.

Most websites are far from clear about their positioning. Once we talk to the business owner we find out why: their positioning isn't clear in their own minds yet.

Here are some questions to help you clarify your positioning:

- Who is your primary competitor, and how are they different to you?
- What does your exact target customer look like? How are they different to your competitor's target customer?
- What's the difference between you and the average business in your market?
- What sort of customer do you turn into a raving fan, while they're unable to get a similar feeling from other providers?
- What annoys your customers about your market?
- What can you do for your customers that no one else can? What keeps them coming back to you over your rivals?

Once you are clear on your positioning it should shine through everything you do, from the copy in your adverts to the tone of your email communications and the text on your website. Not everyone will be a good fit for your positioning, and that's OK. You shouldn't be afraid of disqualifying unsuitable customers as much as attracting your ideal customer. If it were possible to be everything to everyone, there would only be one business in the entire world.

Profile your Perfect Customer (PC)

Profitable marketing is usually about limiting wastage. Wastage comes from taking a shotgun approach, blasting out a message in the general direction of some people and hoping to make a sale. By being more focussed (a sniper rifle vs shotgun) we can take every Pound, Dollar or Euro and spend it talking only to laser targeted potential customers, multiplying the effectiveness of the same budget.

Most of the businesses we help were previously spending a significant portion of their marketing budget talking to customers who wouldn't or *couldn't* buy from them. Taking this cash and focussing it more narrowly at likely potential customers sounds so basic, and yet so few make this a priority.

It's a variation of the 80/20 rule: 20% of their customers produce 80% of their revenue, which leaves the other 80% of their customers contributing only 20% of the revenue. Imagine what happens when we focus the marketing message on attracting *more* of the sort of customers in the valuable 20% group rather than trying to cast a wider, less targeted net.

The first step is to identify what sets the most valuable 20% apart. Usually this group buys in larger volume, is happy to pay premium prices and/or comes back again and again to make repeat purchases. These are the questions we find useful to help profile the Perfect Customer:

- How do you know your best customers are your best customers? What makes them so good?
- Can you spot them as soon as they walk in the door or make contact? If so, what is it about them that identifies them to you?
- What is it about your business that most attracts them?
- How can you amplify this and give them more of what they want?
- Are there parts of your message that risk alienating them? For example focussing on being the lowest price to those customers for whom great service is the only thing that matters?

Similarly, identify those customers who are in the least profitable 80% group. They are the bulk of your customer list, and they give you three options:

1. Focus on bringing them into your most profitable 20% group through upselling additional products or services to them.
2. Leave them be, but adjust your marketing message to attract more of the top producing

group in future and gradually shift the balance of high return customers to low-return customers.

3. Jettison them to free up time and resources to focus purely on your best customers and attracting more of them.

Your choice depends on your business and your comfort levels.

Fire Your Least Profitable Customers

Every business has their share of nightmare customers. The ones who call up every day with questions you've already answered; they request refunds on products but continue to buy from you (only to request further refunds), and they generally suck the life from you or your team. Whoever said 'the Customer is Always Right' had certainly never worked in customer service...

The best approach for such customers is to politely tell them that you are unable to serve them in the manner that they require, then recommend your closest competitor as a suitable alternative. This frees you up to spend time serving and attracting more PCs.

Nowhere is it written that you have to serve every customer who walks through the door, and nor is it good for team moral. Let them go and bog someone else down instead.

Use PR as Free Advertising

interesting information they're after, they will gladly use it.

The approach that *doesn't* work so well is the typical PR approach used by most companies who dabble. They publish press releases with titles like "Company X announces product Y. Now 12% faster and with faster response time..." Boring, overly promotional, valueless drivel, and nobody cares. Even if you manage to find an editor that will print this type of thing, it doesn't get read and it certainly doesn't generate much excitement or interest amongst readers (your ultimate target audience).

Obviously the most effective ads focus on the customer and the *benefits* of your product or service, and a press release or article should be no different. The stories with the highest chance of publication are those that provide a new insight, recommendations or advice for readers or viewers, a timely survey or perhaps analysis on something current.

We're not saying you can't talk about your new product or service. Of course there should be a self promotional component, otherwise we are simply freelance writers or interviewees working for free. But their has to be an angle that is of interest to the audience in order to get the story published and read.

For first time PR writers, it can be difficult to find an angle for your story that will be interesting and relevant to your target audience. Have you noticed a particular trend in their buying patterns (fashion)? Do you have some recommendations for them to avoid some common mistakes, thus positioning your business as the helpful expert? If you are announcing a new product, service or business, what sort of interesting stories can you tell about why you are launching it? Is there a large unmet need which you seek to meet, or is there something that places you perfectly to help a particular type of customer? Do you personally have a story that others would find motivational or inspirational? Careful with this one though - you've probably noticed that our own stories can be disproportionately fascinating to ourselves.

Once you have chosen your angle, it's time to do some outreach. Whenever we are getting an article or news item published, we'll draw up a list of suitable outlets and pitch them a slightly different variation of the idea. This allows us to offer each of them exclusivity on that particular story, which dramatically increases the likelihood of it being placed. We'll research and contact the most suitable person - usually by email, sometimes by phone - offering the story and asking if they think it would be of interest to their readers.

If you have an attractive angle and the editor can see how the readers would find your story interesting, you'll often get a positive response asking you to send over the article. This is when you write the article and send it over. We've found this two step approach to be much more effective than sending the article cold. The offer of exclusivity is also a differentiator as these folk are used to being blasted an email with 100 other poorly-selected contacts in the CC: line.

Once an editor has requested your article, do the work properly and write or prepare it in a way that fits with the style of the publication. Use a similar word count and language to other published articles so that minimal editing is required. If you send over a half-finished piece that requires extensive rewriting, it's far less appealing than a ready to publish finished article. If it needs to be proof read, then hire a proofreader. Give it your very best shot and work as if it really matters. Trust us, it won't go unnoticed with the editor.

If you're writing for a magazine or newspaper, try to include an image that they can use alongside the story. Where possible it should be original, because this eliminates any copyright or licensing issues. If you have to use a stock photo, be careful to explain to the editor exactly where you got the photo from and, if possible, link them to the terms of the license. Again the aim is to make publishing your article an extremely simple and desirable proposition. The more work you require the publication to do (including sourcing a suitable picture), the more you decrease the likelihood of them running the piece.

You'll obviously want to include an element of promotion in your article, and you can approach this in two ways:

Free Advertising/Lead Generation

We have built two entire businesses on the back of lead generation campaigns run through articles written for magazines. The articles provide insight or advice about a particular subject of interest to the reader, then offer a free gift to readers. They are invited to text or visit a website to claim their free gift, and we then use these contact details to market to them. The free gift itself is usually a piece of promotional material with enough valuable information contained in it for it to have high perceived value.

By using press in this way, we're essentially getting highly effective advertising, free of charge and disguised as articles. The quality of the articles is so high that they attract readers, and by offering a tantalising offer at the end we're making sure that we motivate the readers to action (giving us their contact details).

Of course, some publications will smell a rat with this approach and see that you're just sneaking in some free advertising under the radar. Most won't though, and they'll happily run your ads free of charge.

For those that do protest at your inclusion of an offer, you can strike a deal to run a paid advert as well, in return for the article's inclusion. Don't fall for the 'minimum of 5 insertions' rule to 'build familiarity', but instead tell the magazine that you're testing the effectiveness of the ad using a lead generation offer, so you'll immediately be able to gauge the response rate.

Positioning and Awareness

The softer approach to running a lead generation press campaign is to try and build awareness of your product or service with the hope that readers or viewers will take action on their own accord to become customers. While this is much easier than designing and running a lead generation campaign, it's also generally much less effective and will generate far fewer direct customers.

Pitching for TV Coverage

If you're aiming for TV or online video coverage, do everything you can to show your contact that you'd make a good interviewee. Send a short and well-lit video of yourself in front of the camera appearing comfortable and relaxed. Make sure you know what you're going to be saying, and your lines are well enough rehearsed that they sound natural and you can focus more on the delivery than what you're actually saying.

Follow up

The folks receiving articles and emails for press coverage tend to be extremely busy and deluged with emails, so it's a good idea to send a follow up after a couple of working days if you haven't heard back from them. Politely ask if they received your work, and if they had any feedback as to whether it would be the sort of thing their audience would be interested in. We find that it's almost *always* only through the follow up that we get a response from the editor, so it's important to be diligent about it.

Thank anyone who offers to run the piece and remember to ask for a copy of the publication. Your appearance in recognised publications is useful to put on your website and use in your marketing as a credibility tool, so remember to blog and tweet about it once it's live.

The Online Effect

While our exploration of PR as a source of new business and free advertising has mostly focussed on the offline world, this being an online marketing guide we'll also need to take a look at how we can leverage PR to boost your online profile.

Most of the print publications you might be targeting as part of your offline PR campaign will have an online counterpart, whether it's a full online version of the print magazine, or a companion website. Most of the time, these counterpart websites or online publications still get a fraction of the readership of the print versions, but they have a couple of major advantages. The first is backlinks, which we'll look at in more detail in the section on SEO. Backlinks are still the core currency of search ranking, and can be very beneficial to any business wanting to increase it's search engine visibility. Prominent publication websites tend to have high online authority, so backlinks from these types of sites are very desirable.

The second advantage is that the visitors who are interested in your product or service can click straight through to your website. Clicking on a link on an open webpage is obviously far less effort than putting down a physical magazine, going to a computer and typing in a web address.

To generate online press exposure, follow exactly the same procedure as for print or TV. If you're offering an article or press release for a physical publication, don't forget to offer it for their website as well in order to snap up these online-specific benefits. The ultimate in this regard is print magazines that have a free-to-view online version with live links.

Find PR Opportunities Online

There are plenty of places that businesses looking to generate press can go online to find such opportunities. Every day, busy and overworked journalists and editors are trying to fill their publications and find interviewees to beef up their articles. This type of promotion is on so few of your competitors' radars that it can be incredibly easy to secure it.

Journalist enquiry services (also called media enquiry services) are services that journalists use to put out requests for businesses and PRs to talk to or interview for their articles or TV features. Subscribers (and there is usually a cost for the best quality services) receive notifications by email of any enquiries that come in matching the criteria they have selected.

Let's look at an example:

Kate runs a shop that sells boutique lighting, and she wants to promote her e-commerce store through some well targeted press exposure. She subscribes to a media enquiry service and chooses the Interiors and Home category, indicating the type of enquiry that she is interested in.

She then starts to receive requests from journalists looking for businesses that can provide content, including one from a TV production company looking for products to feature in a home renovations show - the sort of enquiry that is fairly typical in this type of category. Kate responds and finds out that she would need to provide any products free of charge, but that they would be featured on the TV show's website and her company's website would be appear briefly on the show. She decides that for the cost of the lights this is a great investment.

For the cost of the lighting, Kate has secured:

- Placement in a TV show
- A link to her e-commerce store from the TV show website
- Positioning of her products in front of a qualified target audience (those interested in interior design)

How else can Kate take advantage? As her lighting has appeared on the TV show, she can now use the channel and TV show's logos on her website. This boosts her store's credibility and increases trust amongst visitors new to the site. If Kate wants to leverage the appearance still further, she can use the story of appearing on the show in other publications, for example local newspapers. Local newspapers are so desperate for content that, with a good angle, she stands a good chance of getting some coverage in a 'local girl done good' type of piece.

Industry Magazines and Blogs

You'd be amazed at how easy it can be to get a regular, high visible blog on high profile magazine websites in your industry. Every market has them, whether they're online only or the website companion to the most popular magazines.

Every blog editor knows that they need plenty of good quality content for their blog, and they also know that paying their own team to write it is expensive. Worse, it's not always easy to get really good quality content 'straight from the frontline'. Professional writers are usually a little insulated from the action, and yet they are expected to be the fountain of knowledge to an audience made up of the *real* experts. You, on the other hand, are well positioned to offer a unique perspective on your industry, and if you show that you're sympathetic to the writing style and target audience, you can quickly become the blog editor's best friend.

So how do you go about securing a regular blog?

The first step is outreach to the editor. We usually recommend offering just a single article to begin with, in much the same as you would if you were pitching a magazine article. This builds familiarity and shows the editor that you can work quickly and your writing is of a good standard. Once they've published the article, it's important to thank them and mention what sort of response you've had from the blog audience (clue: it's best to let them know the response was "unbelievable", even if it was unbelievably *bad*). This is the best time to suggest that you write a follow up piece, and to hint that perhaps you could look at making it a more regular blog as you have plenty to offer on the subject.

If they agree, they might suggest that you submit pieces at a certain interval. Left to its own devices this interval will invariably grow wider and wider as time goes on, so if at all possible stick it in the calendar and book an appointment with yourself to write your blog post each month.

As with any PR outreach attempts, the key is volume. If you rely on contacting only one site, you'll probably be disappointed when they don't reply. If you set a goal to contact 5-10 sites, you're much more likely to get at least one of them agree.

Finding PR opportunities online is ongoing work that you can do in the background of your online social life. Each time you find a relevant publication or blog, drop them a line and keep a note of it in a press schedule. We find that a simple spreadsheet with the name of the publication, key contact, date of first contact, date of follow ups and date of expected publication (once they've agreed) allows you to keep your press exposure organised. It's a useful tool allowing you to schedule your different promotions through the quarter so you're not hit by unexpected spikes in demand.

The opportunities are out there, and the vast majority of your competitors are doing absolutely nothing about them. Don't be one of them, and make sure that you have an online-PR component in your 2014 marketing plan.

Use Trackable Numbers to Measure Each of Your Marketing Channels

Most businesses involved in online marketing can probably identify with John Wanamaker, who is reported to have said "half the money I spend on advertising is wasted; the trouble is I don't know which half." While John was overall pretty ad-savvy (he is reported to have 'invented' the money back guarantee), his 50% wastage could have been avoided by a simple solution available to every business owner in the world today for the price of a very average restaurant meal.

Trackable phone numbers are one of the most useful ROI-enhancing marketing tools available, but because they're not particularly 'sexy' they don't get talked about very often. Their inner beauty comes from their ability to precisely track the effectiveness of marketing pieces that generate phone calls rather than clicks.

A trackable number is simply a virtual number with the same local code as your current number, but it's not connected to its own physical line. Most businesses set up their virtual numbers to forward calls on to their regular phone number, allowing them to answer the phone exactly the same, but with the additional benefit of an online dashboard showing how many calls their virtual number is receiving. By creating and assigning a number of different virtual phone numbers to different marketing channels, you can track the effectiveness of each: flyers, websites, magazine articles and Adwords extensions are all now as trackable as links on a page. Now you can judge the exact conversion rate of each marketing piece that would otherwise be left to guesswork.

There are a huge number of trackable numbers services and it's worth paying for a service that takes on all of the set up for you, as this can be quite messy.

You can also set up a VOIP service that shows you the source of the call, so if your sales team needs to respond to a particular offer on a certain number, they can have that information in front of them ready.

See our website for more information about our trackable numbers service, or drop us a line if you need some help.

Use vouchers to drive engagement

There are three main reasons to use vouchers as part of your marketing:

1. They are a great way to make a specific offer which can channel people into your most profitable or desirable product or service.
2. You can use voucher codes to you can see where voucher traffic has come from (this is known as 'keying' an ad).
3. They're a great way to introduce your business to new customers, as they encourage the customer to focus on the value of the voucher rather than the risk of buying something unproven.

4. (Bonus reason) You'll activate the powerful 'bargain gland' in people

Let's look through the reasons in turn:

Channel people to a product or service of your choice

If your business is such that there is a particular product or service that suits new buyers (an introductory offer, for example an accountant offering a tax return service to small businesses) you can use vouchers to channel them into this purchase, and from there you can upsell them (to monthly management accounting services, for example).

If you have a good base of existing customers, vouchers can be used to move these guys up to the next level or sell follow-on products. A car garage can make an offer to their existing MOT customers for a special winter maintenance package, for example.

For businesses that don't offer discrete fixed products (for example consultancy or training businesses) you can bundle these into a packaged 'widget' which can then be promoted using vouchers. For example, personal trainers selling 'New Years Get Fit' packages, rather than selling only one off sessions.

Use voucher codes to measure traffic sources

It's important to know which sources of traffic are working most effectively for you, and by using unique voucher codes for each of your online channels, you'll be able to see how many people find you through each source. Your Facebook voucher code can be different to your Google+ voucher code and different again to your website voucher code. If your instructions require customers to ring or email quoting the voucher code to claim their discount or gift, you'll be able to simply tally the number of each voucher claimed to assess the effectiveness of each channel in the promotion.

Introduce your business to new customers

The period when potential customers are researching you and your competitors is crucial to your success or failure. Get the initial attraction phase right, you have a chance to show this customer what you're really like, impress them with your service and hopefully keep them for life. Lose out in this attraction phase to a competitor, and you're left relying on them failing to keep that customer if you're to get a second chance.

A well timed and attractive voucher can tip the scales in your favour and entice that 'on the edge' customer to give you a chance. If you know the numbers in your business and are willing to play the long game, you'll be surprised how *valuable* an offer you can afford to make to obtain each new customer. Offering a free gift with first purchase, a significant discount on their first order or another introductory bonus will help get them in the door, handing over their payment details and taking their way to being a repeat customer.

One of our clients runs a very successful dental practice and uses an introductory voucher in conjunction with a lead generation campaign with great success. He offers a £15 check up to new patients if they sign up to the practice mailing list. This price is significantly cheaper than his competitors and means that the surgery makes very little money on the checkups. But because he understands the long term value of these customers, it's an offer he's happy to make all day every day. Not only does the voucher bring the practice new customers, but it also allows the staff to track the leads coming from the website. While his competitors might turn their noses up at appearing to leave money on the table by offering such a discounted check up, Chig knows that this is money invested in acquiring new customers. And that's the best money you can spend.

Work out how much you can spend to acquire a customer

The most intelligent marketing decisions have very little to do with creativity, or flair, but instead are based on a cold and rational understanding of some key numbers. One of the most important numbers that every business should know is their maximum acceptable cost to acquire a new customer. Trying to make marketing decisions *without* knowing your acceptable cost per acquisition is like shooting at a target blindfolded.

One of the key areas your competitors probably limit their marketing (and therefore their success) is that they're likely unwilling to spend much money acquiring each new customer. Without working out their maximum cost per acquisition, most people make overly conservative marketing decisions, unnecessarily limiting the reach and appeal of their marketing, promotions and front end offers. This gives you a very exciting opportunity to snatch potential customers from right under their noses.

Working out your existing cost per customer acquisition is easy: divide the cost of your marketing by the number of new customers it brings. You'll then see how much each new customer is costing from each of your marketing channels.

Next, to help you work out what an acceptable maximum cost per acquisition is, work out your average lifetime customer value as in the previous step. To do this, multiply your average profit per transaction by the average number of transactions per customer. For some businesses (wedding dress shops, laser eye surgery clinics) their average number of transactions will tend towards one, but for most others there will be a significant amount of repeat business.

What should emerge from calculating your average lifetime customer value is that you can actually afford to spend a lot more money attracting a customer than you might make on the first sale alone. If a house cleaning company on average books 5 cleanings per customer making $40 profit each time, they should be willing to spend considerably more than $40 to attract a new customer. They might decide to offer a free $50 shopping voucher for each new customer, knowing that on average they're still going to come away with $150 profit over that customer's lifetime ($40 x 5 transactions minus the $50 cost of the voucher). The incentive of the $50 voucher will significantly increase their conversion rate, bringing them more customers and making them far more money overall.

Alternatively they might offer a free window cleaning service worth $50 (that in fact only costs them $20 to fulfil). Not only will this incentivise new sales, but provides an excellent opportunity to upsell the window cleaning service thus increasing the value of that client.

Most businesses would react in horror at the thought of spending more on getting a customer than the value of the first sale ("going negative on the front end"), but as you can see it's a perfectly rational long term strategy. Businesses that can afford to outspend their competitors in marketing and front end offers are in an extremely strong competitive position.

As a final illustration, the 7 Point Marketing Reviews we offer readers at http://exposureninja.com/101 take our highly-trained experts 2-3 hours to complete on average, and they're more in-depth than audits costing £200+ from the other less rigorous marketing companies. However, the level of detail and the quality of the information leads a significant number of review requesters to become clients of ours, and over time we'll recoup this initial investment. Because we know our numbers it's something we're happy to do.

Being willing to spend more than your customers to acquire a new customer gives you a valuable competitive advantage and allows you to grow your business as fast as *you* like, rather than relying on market conditions or the actions of your competitors.

Use your personality to sell more

All else being equal, we'd all prefer to do business with somebody we know and trust. Despite this so many business owners shy away from recognition and instead try to cultivate the appearance of a large faceless corporation.

As humans we seem to be programmed to identify and build relationships with other human beings; we'll pay a higher price for a brand associated with a celebrity or familiar figure, for example, even if their area of core expertise is totally unrelated to the product they are associated with. Visible founders or businesses with a familiar face can attract valuable press exposure because people are more curious about another human than they are about a nondescript anonymous brand. Richard Branson is not an aeroplane, train or finance expert and yet some people will trust his company more than his competitors because of their familiarity with him.

What we're really talking about is tapping into a type of *celebrity*. But it's not the celebrity that is characterised by champagne and drunken brawls, but rather credibility, familiarity and authority. Any business owner can develop these traits in their market, but to do so they have to be willing to step into the spotlight and hop up onto the podium. If you wait until the world recognises you for your expertise and authority, you'll be waiting a long time. Instead you've got to be willing to proclaim yourself the expert. There really is no anointing ceremony other than the one you organise yourself.

A lot of the marketing and promotional tips in this book can be built around the personality of you, the business owner, whether it's starting a blog, writing some articles for respected magazines, publishing a book or simply adding more personality to the content on your website.

Your website is a really good place to start adding some sprinkles of personality because it's your first touch point for a lot of people. Everything you say on your site should be personal to your business and emphasising the benefits to your customer in the language you would use if you were talking to them face to face. Generic and impersonal content has its place, but it doesn't drive sales so that place shouldn't be on your website.

One of the reasons people give for not using their personality in their business is that they want to sell the business once it's large enough. They worry that the value will be affected by the loss of the figurehead. This is a legitimate concern, but allowing it to prevent you from growing your business in the first place doesn't make much sense. Build first then, once you're ready to sell, the transition can be handled sensitively. Limiting your growth to make selling easier later on is like refusing to go on holiday because you don't like having to return home.

Another fear that business owners have is that they worry their personality won't come across or that they'll turn customers off. The key thing to remember here is that you use what you've got. If you're not a confident public speaker, just having your face on the website or advertising material gives potential customers reassurance that someone is willing to be accountable. Have someone on the team who is good with writing to create the articles or content on your behalf. If you're outgoing and lively, consider running some seminars, making videos or engaging publicly on social media with your audience.

Once you've experimented with making yourself more visible and your audience has responded well to it, this'll help give you more confidence to ramp up the personality in your business.

Run a Newsletter Service

Most of your competitors will skip over this tip. Just from the headline it sounds too much like hard work, not particularly sexy and like it will probably cost money. They'd be right on all three assumptions!

Newsletters might sound a bit old school to appear in a book about up-to-the-minute Internet Marketing, but that's precisely why they can work so well.

Sending your customers and leads a newsletter every month or two has three main benefits:

1. It positions you in your field. The business that sends out the newsletter covering the breaking news in their industry, relevant information, and some entertainment for good measure is perceived very differently to the invisible business that lives totally under the radar. Who sends out Newsletters? Only current and high authority businesses.
2. It keeps you in your audience's minds. A posted newsletter in particular is something that's quite difficult to ignore. Not everyone will read it cover to cover, but everyone who receives it will be thinking about you.
3. You can use it as a selling platform. Seasonal offers, exclusive deals and special bundles for

newsletter 'members' can drive purchases. Interviews and case studies with existing customers, information about trends and new products, referral incentives... your newsletter is a chance to get some quality one-on-one time with your audience away from the computer.

Making sure that your newsletter gets read frequently is the difference between *investing* in a successful marketing channel and spending time and money sending out something headed straight for the recycling bin. The key to getting your newsletter read is (just like all customer communication) to focus on how you can use it to move your audience closer to their goals.

If the first issue your customer receives helps them in some way get closer to the result they really want, you'll get a chance to reach them in their second issue, and so on. Your goal is to make your audience think of your communications as 'must read', and it takes time to build this trust. Always focusing on making your audience happy is the quickest way to get them to prioritise your communications.

Just like with email communication, the frequency of your newsletter is also an important consideration. Optimum frequency will depend on your business and audience, but judgements about frequency should be made by talking to customers and testing rather than assumptions that your audience doesn't want to hear from you. It's true, people might not be ready for a newsletter from their accountant every fortnight. But on the other hand, if that accountant's newsletter is dedicated to saving the reader money by reducing bills and getting the best deals on the things they buy, that information could easily justify a valuable monthly newsletter.

If you're stuck for content, here are some nice time- and creativity saving shortcuts taken from our own experience running various newsletter businesses:

- Interviews with high profile figures in your industry can be carried out quickly, and if by email, don't require you to do very much writing. What's more, the power of association boosts your own credibility.
- 'Trend watch' articles about what's hot and what's up and coming allow you to position yourself on the cutting edge.
- Reviews of products, services, events and anything else relevant to your audience is not only interesting to them, but if your readership is sizable or particularly well-targeted, you can some great free stuff out of it too.
- 'This month in…' behind the scenes content not related to your audience, but about your business or your life build the personality and familiarity in your business. Keep it aspirational, positive and aligned to your audience.
- Educational articles teaching your customers or prospects something that will move them closer towards their goals always proves popular, and

don't be scared of 'giving too much away' - focus on giving as much as possible and you'll get plenty in return.

- Customer/client of the month is a mutually beneficial article. An interview and story with one of your most successful or high profile clients is a great chance to showcase the benefits of additional products or services that you sell through real life examples, as well as making them feel special.

Your newsletter doesn't have to be a slick, glossy masterpiece. The most important part (aside from the basic fact that you're *doing* it) is the content, and if it looks a little homemade that's perfectly fine. The personality behind the business is an important part of why the newsletter model works so well, so a simply-formatted newsletter stapled in the corner is more consistent in this regard than an expensive brochure-type mailing which screams "generic" and is less likely to pass the tricky 'Straight Into the Recycling Bin' test.

Paid Newsletter services

If your audience is really hungry for information, a paid newsletter service can be a very good source of additional continuity (recurring) income. The rules for content and presentation are exactly the same as a free newsletter service, because you're always trying to provide as much value to your audience as possible.

Attracting paying subscribers is more about the angle and quality of the pitch than the content you're offering. As long as you can clearly demonstrate that your members will receive more value each issue than the cost of the newsletter, you shouldn't find it hard to convert subscribers that are familiar with you. Enticing introductory offers and bundling in your core products or services can incentivise people to sign up, and you'll be surprised how long they stay paying members once they're in the habit of receiving the newsletter.

One of the most crucial elements of a recurring business like this is automatic payments. If you require your subscribers to pay an invoice each month, you'll find yourself chasing payments and losing subscribers who decide one month that they'd rather do without the expense. If the payments are made automatically, you'll average a far higher member lifetime because people simply can't be bothered to turn off the payments.

One final tip: in our experience you'll find it a lot easier to sell a *physical* newsletter service than an e-newsletter service. We are all flooded with emails, and for many people the idea of yet more email sounds like a nuisance. A physical paper newsletter has far higher perceived value, and despite the extra effort you'll find it to be far more profitable because it actually gets read.

Build a customer email list

Collecting the email addresses of existing customers and sending them emails is a game changer for most businesses, but few do it and *very* few do it well.

You've heard the stats about how much easier and cheaper it is to sell to existing customers than attract new ones, but as marketers we all love the rush of generating new business from new clients. Going back to old customers can feel a bit boring, not to mention awkward at first, trying to resell people who have already bought. *"Surely they know where to find me if they want me?"*

But for almost any business (there are rare exceptions) their existing customer base is a vast untapped potential source of sales that is just too rich to be ignored.

The key to building your list is making it a process that happens almost automatically. We helped one of our restaurant clients implement the email list method by providing them with an iPad and app that they hand to guests at the end of their meal. The guests are asked to submit feedback about the meal as well as their name, email address and birthday. Armed with this, the restaurant can now keep in touch with these customers throughout the year, and send special promotion offers in their birthday month to attract the lucrative special occasion bookings.

Without the email list, they'd be restricted to the back end/repeat business 'marketing strategies' of their competitors: opening the door and hoping for these previous customers to walk in. With the email list, they're able to proactively market to their fans and run midweek promotions, for example, to keep the restaurant busy during times that would usually be quiet.

Run an email list for prospects

Of course you don't have to stop there. Setting up an email list for *potential* customers that haven't bought yet is just as powerful, and can help you convert more website visitors and enquiries into new customers.

Another of our clients runs an email list to entice website visitors to give her training school a try. It's a crowded market, and with the proliferation of online learning and free training via YouTube, it can be a tough sell. Because the quality of their training is so high, we decided that the best advertising for the training was the training itself. So we set up an email capture form on her website offering a voucher for a 'taster' training course. The taster training is held at the training school and with the same instructors as the regular training, so it gives the potential customer the complete experience of what they'd get as someone on the main training course. They get a chance to meet the other students, the instructor and find out more about the main course and have a chance to book on right there and then.

The beauty of running an email list for *potential* clients like this is that you have a chance to build a relationship with them over time and away from the noise of your competitors' websites. When people are in the research phase, they might be looking through dozens of different competing websites and trawling through an overwhelming amount of information. Then the dog bites the postman and the cat is sick on the crying baby. They close the laptop to resume their research at a later date, and your website leaves their consciousness

But if they signed up to your email list, you have the opportunity to educate them further on your business in the meantime. You can give them a taste of the benefits they'll receive, and build familiarity. When it comes time for them to make a decision, they've been receiving your emails and are subsequently more familiar with you than any of your competitors. You are the 'safe' choice and the clear favourite going into the final round, all thanks to your email list...

The mechanics of setting up an email list

There are 2 basic options for running your email list: DIY or pro.

THE DIY EMAIL LIST

Piecing together your business email account, email software like Outlook or OSX's Mail, or using a web-based email system like Gmail, it's possible to run a basic email list free of charge and without having to learn anything new.

You can simply collect email addresses in a spreadsheet, copy them into the BCC line of a new email, and send this out to your 'subscribers'. It's quick, simple and does the job if you don't want to take the plunge with an autoresponder service.

While it doesn't offer the extended functionality of an autoresponder, it has the advantage of being free. But Autoresponders offer some significant benefits for those willing to spend a small amount.

The Pro email list: Autoresponders

An autoresponder allows you to manage your email list more effectively, as well as automating the collection of new subscribers. Using an autoresponder service like Aweber or Mailchimp you can set up different lists (one of prospects, one for existing customers for example), create automated email sequences, track your audience's clicks, segment your lists and use all sorts of other fancy and useful list management features to save you time and enable you to sell more effectively.

Collecting your customers' and potential customers' email addresses is done through simple forms, and these can be placed on your website, on social sites or anywhere else that you might want to collect email addresses. Through displaying unsubscribe options and use of double optin (requiring your sign ups to confirm their subscription) they also comply with spam laws and free you up from having to deal with unsubscribers manually.

For anyone serious about running a profitable email list then, a professional autoresponder service is a good investment and will free you up from the basic email list management tasks to work on the higher-value stuff, such as planning the email strategy and focussing on attracting more subscribers. It's all too easy to spend a few hours trying to 'save' a few dollars, without realising that your time is far too valuable to spend doing these basic tasks when other more profitable marketing activities require your attention.

Throughout the rest of this book we'll look at strategies to help you profit from your email list, but deciding to invest the time setting up your list is one of the most important internet marketing decisions you can make.

Sell effectively to your email list

Once you've setup your email list (or lists), you'll want to start making some money out of it. Obviously the approach varies depending on whether your list is of prospects, customers or a combination of both. The overall goals are the same though: build familiarity and trust to motivate purchases.

The bulk of your email communication should be focussed on (yes, you've guessed it) moving your audience closer to their goals. Repeatedly bludgeoning your audience with the 'buy our stuff' hammer is a surefire way to knock the rapport out of them, and once it's gone, it's difficult to get back.

The trick is to mix the 'buy our stuff' message with useful and valuable content. How can you help your buyers to get the most out of their purchases? Can you give prospects tips to help them choose between apparently similar options? What are the common mistakes to avoid in their situation?

Then of course there is the credibility- and authority-building content: testimonials and case studies, if presented properly, can be interesting and valuable to your audience as well as help to drive sales.

Time specific offers and launches

Product launches can be a very powerful way to bring in a significant amount of cash in over a short period of time. By building up anticipation and educating your audience over a period of weeks, you can move a significant chunk of your audience to buy, using the 'herd effect' to build excitement and drive more sales.

If you're running a time-specific offer (for example restaurants running high-priced Valentine's day promotions or a personal trainer opening a limited number of places for an exciting new program), plan out the launch strategy in advance to start 'warming up' your audience.

Running a separate lead generation campaign to an *existing* email list can be a good way to separate those who are *really* keen so that you can laser focus the promotional message and make sure you're targeting the right audience with your offer. This way you know *who* to invest the most time in selling to without putting off those who aren't qualified to buy: the restaurant doesn't want to expend too much energy and risk annoying their single customers by hammering them with the Valentine's day emails, for example. So running a separate lead generation campaign to their whole list offering a free guide to 'What women *really* want on Valentine's day - 5 steps to the perfect Valentine's evening' can allow them to build a separate list of only those potentially interested in booking a Valentine's meal.

In running our own launches for training and information products, we've found an approach that mixes email and direct mail to be very effective. We'll tend to send short emails to prepare the ground for a longer-form posted sales letter for the offer. Getting someone to read 2,000 words in an email is tough, but it's surprisingly easy when put in a catchy direct mail piece.

List segmentation

Segmenting your email list according to their characteristics and purchases allows you to match your message to different audiences, maximising the response. Although you can do this segmentation manually, automation rules inside the autoresponder software allows you to set this up automatically.

One of the businesses we run has 4 different levels of customer list for a single product:

1. Prospects are those who joined the email list in order to get information about the product. These guys and gals receive emails positioning us, demonstrating expertise and trying to get them to 'move up' to the next level.

2. Leads are those who responded to an additional lead generation campaign run to this list. We offered a free information guide by post if people fill in a form with their address details. This form also captured their name and email address again, and the autoresponder then removed them from the prospects list and put them in a new leads list, allowing us to automate follow up about the information guide. We know that we can contact these guys a bit more aggressively because they've expressed a level of interest above that of those who stay in the prospects list.

3. Customer list. Once someone buys the product, the payment processor (Paypal in this case) automatically removes them from the leads list and adds them to the customer list. They then stop receiving sales emails and begin receiving

follow up, satisfaction and upsell emails advertising the monthly club.

4. Continuity customer list. This product had an additional monthly 'club' that buyers could join if they paid a monthly fee. Those who bought the upsell to the monthly club need to receive a different set of emails to those who didn't, so their purchase of the monthly package automatically moves them to the fourth and final list.

It's like a series of sieves, filtering out river sludge to find precious gold. Each sieve contains has a progressively higher quality customer, until the final sieve contains only the gold. You can invest more time and energy polishing this gold up to a bright sheen without having to polish every rock and grain of sand in the first sieve.

A well-maintained email list can be your business's greatest asset, and once a system is in place to collect and nurture these leads and customers, it can work on autopilot 24/7/365 without any effort on your part. Lead capture and automated follow up allow you to leverage your sales process and get on with running your business, while customers are automatically moved closer to the all-important purchase.

Use Risk Reversal to boost conversions

When asking a new customer to do business with them, most businesses demand that the customer takes on the risk. Whether walking into a restaurant, clicking 'Proceed to checkout', picking up the phone, or any other *pull the trigger* actions, the customer needs to have enough confidence in their decision to outweigh any misgivings or doubts they might have, even if these misgivings are inaccurate or exaggerated.

For example, visitors to an old fashioned or amateurish website might feel that the business is not well established or is untrustworthy. These visitors might also be uneducated about your market and fail to understand why a particular service you offer is at a different price to your competitors. They might not truly understand what it is that they're buying, and how suitable it is in their specific circumstances.

While it is the aim of your website and marketing materials to try to answer and minimise these doubts, the doubts themselves are outside of your control and will always exist to some extent. Besides, for every person who buys from or contacts you, how many more *nearly* did but their doubts got the better of them?

By using Risk Reversal and guarantees, you can remove the customer's risk, and take it on yourself. You're offering to put your money where your mouth is: "this is good, I know it's good and I'm so confident that you'll think so too, that I'll buy it back if you don't agree."

The most common risk reversal tool is the standard 'money back guarantee'. A money back guarantee is a very powerful sales tool for any business that can offer it, and in some markets it's difficult doing business without it.

But the trouble with the money back guarantee is that it can sometimes blend into the background, so to make the guarantee stand out you can add some spice. Here's a story to illustrate how Tim spiced up standard guarantees and turned them into selling points:

In one of my first businesses I was selling a DVD course through email and direct mail. I had written, filmed and edited it myself, and it *looked like it* too. I was duplicating the DVDs on my laptop and printing the covers on my desktop printer. If that doesn't sound like enough of a struggle, I was selling them for £400 (about $600) when other DVDs in that market were professionally filmed, looked much slicker and sold for less than £20. Just to make it more challenging, my target audience was musicians in their early to mid 20s. In other words I was selling an expensive product with low quality presentation to people with no money.

The good news was that I had marketing on my side, and the three guarantees I offered managed to offset the elements that were stacked against me. My three guarantees were:
1. Standard money back guarantee. This is a default catch-all that stated that if the buyer was unhappy with the course *for any reason*, they could return it for a full 100% refund of every

penny they paid (the redundancy was intentional for emphasis). The buyers had a full <u>year</u> to make this decision, and we'll talk about why that's important shortly.

2. A results-based guarantee. The course showed musicians how to make money from their music through marketing themselves effectively. I knew two things: 1) that if people followed the steps in the course, they'd make a LOT of money (I had done it myself), and 2) that most people who bought the course would not do a single thing. That's not because they're lazy, but because they're human. OK, so it's because they're lazy. The results-based guarantee that I made was "Earn back 5 times your investment in 4 months". The caveat was that they had to show me that they'd implemented the steps in the course. This would prevent people requesting a refund without taking any action. This type of guarantee just *screams* confidence in your product. For those in two minds about the effectiveness of the strategies I was teaching, here was a clear sign that I was willing to put my money where my mouth was.

3. The final guarantee is the one I was most proud of. The '£100,000 Guarantee' I offered really stood out to an audience who had never dealt with anything like that amount of money. The guarantee stated that if the buyer didn't believe the course content would be worth a *minimum* of £100,000 to them during their lifetime, I'd refund

them. The truth is that good marketing is worth vastly more than £100,000 to people that implement it or have it implemented for them. Combine this with the enthusiasm and optimism people feel when learning something new, and it was virtually impossible to resist. But the wording of the guarantee directly associated the course with an increase of £100,000 to the buyer's bank account. Given the choice between a £20 DVD and a DVD costing 20 times as much but that earns you £100,000, which would you choose?

When it comes to guarantees, you can't go overboard.

This applies in almost any business. Even if the returned products are useless, the benefits of offering powerful guarantees significantly outweighs the cost of fulfilling them.

RISK REVERSAL MISCONCEPTIONS

Businesses that resist risk reversal or have already skipped this section deciding that it's not right for them usually have the same misconceptions. These misconceptions are usually untested and are nearly always wrong:

MISCONCEPTION 1: WE'LL GET A LOT OF REFUNDS

If you're not selling something you're willing to guarantee, find something else to sell. Life is too short to sell crap and deal with unhappy people.

The reality is that if you have a half decent product that does what you claim, the existence of the guarantee won't substantially affect the number of people asking for a refund. Unhappy people will already be telling you they're unhappy, so simply adding a process isn't going to move the needle much.

MISCONCEPTION 2: WE SHOULD OFFER A SHORT REFUND PERIOD TO PREVENT REFUNDS

Tight deadlines cause compliance. Give someone 10 years to do something and if they don't forget (most likely), they won't touch it for 9 years and 11 months. Give them 10 minutes to do it, and they'll jump in now.

The same is true for refunds. The longer you give people to consider their purchase, the fewer refund requests you will get. Give them a week to decide, and if the week ahead looks busy or they're worried that they won't have time to use what they've bought, you're buying it back. Don't force people to make an immediate decision, let them sit with it for a while and consider it more.

Some people don't want to be happy, and nothing you can do is going to alter their course of misery. They're the ones who can find a negative angle in any situation. If you happen to inadvertently sell to one of these types and they ask for a refund, just hand over the cash and cut the cord. Let them drift out into space to bother one of your competitors instead (or, better still, refer them to your most troublesome competitor). It doesn't reflect on your business or the quality of your product, so don't take it personally. There are people out there who would complain about being handed free money, and trying to keep these miserable souls happy is futile.

For many businesses, offering refunds is a legal requirement. If you have to give them to people who ask *anyway*, you might as well use this as a sales tool and get every last drop of marketing value out of them that you possibly can.

Which of the following types of guarantee can you offer, and how can you spice them up?

- Satisfaction guarantee
- Guaranteed results (e.g. *If you don't find a date/lose 10 pounds/learn French fluently etc we'll refund you every penny*).
- Double your money back. If you're really confident in your results, can you offer *more* than your money back? A very powerful guarantee for those that have the confidence to use it. Yes, you'll end up paying some money back to cheapskates, but you'll also make a LOT from real potential customers.
- Price match. If you're the cheapest, guarantee it!
- Service guarantee. If you can guarantee a particular service metric (% uptime, response times etc) then this should be shouted about loud and clear, particular if it addresses an issue in your market.

- Speed of delivery. Many businesses have made speed the core message in their marketing, from FedEx to Dominos pizza. If you pride yourself on speed then it pays to shout about it with a catchy guarantee.

Removing doubt about the buying process

The late, very great Gary Halbert used to talk about how he'd remove the fear for his audience by describing to them exactly what would happen during the buying process. His marketing pieces would tell potential customers precisely what they'd hear during the sales call, what would happen next and what they could expect every step of the way.

For business whose customers are making a one off or new purchase, the uncertainty of how to buy can be off-putting and even intimidating. Walking them through the process step by step removes this uncertainty and gives them confidence that they're making a good choice.

Ask yourself if your audience *really* know what to expect when they buy from you. How could you make this even clearer? Even if you're a standard e-commerce business, an outline of the order process can give reassurance to new orders who perhaps aren't sure when they can expect their order to arrive or how to submit customer service queries.

Make it your goal to remove uncertainty and risk from every possible step in your customer's journey, and you'll be rewarded.

Write your book

While not strictly an online marketing topic, writing a book is a very powerful strategy that can generate a lot of business for you *as part of* your online marketing campaign.

Thanks to Amazon, writing and publishing a book is simpler and easier than ever. Our own book writing process has been fine tuned and we can now go from the planning stage to having a fully fledged book on the bestseller lists in around 6 weeks.

For business owners, it's an incredibly powerful marketing tool. Having a book (and, even better, a bestselling book) is a tremendous credibility tool that gives you bags of authority. It clearly shows your audience that you know what you're talking about and are well established. It's no secret that I built Exposure Ninja almost entirely off the back of the first Google book's success as the volume of enquiries it generated absolutely swamped us and demanded that we hired more help as fast as we could.

Getting Started

What stops most business owners from writing their book is the apparent enormity of the task. Like a non-driver sitting at the steering wheel for the first time, they can't ever imagine a time when the battle ahead would not seem intimidating. Faced with such a huge object, they procrastinate and look to the future waiting for the 'perfect' time to start.

There isn't going to be a perfect time to start. It'll never feel 'just right' and there will always be other things that you need to do. So the best thing to do is get started immediately.

How do you start to write a book? I find a good old Word or Google Drive document to be a good place to start. I'll outline the main sections I want to cover, then break these sections down into points that I want to address. From there you can flesh out the sections as you have time. It makes the whole task more manageable and more like writing lots of mini-guides rather than a huge 45,000 word essay.

Choose your subject carefully

The subject choice is absolutely crucial to your book's success. Just as with all your marketing, your audience is asking 'what's in it for me?' They are not particularly interested in being preached to, told what to think or reminded how incompetent they are.

Your book should, therefore, focus on moving your audience closer to their goals by educating them in a way that makes them feel empowered. Imagine that each of your readers paid $1000 for your book, and it's your job to give them good value for that money. How would you do this and what could you teach them that would earn or save them this money?

Those who are slightly insecure might worry about *giving away the crown jewels* with this approach: "but surely if I tell my audience how to do X they won't hire me to do it for them?"

The truth is that the more high quality information you give your readers, the more they'll trust you and the more they'll see you as an expert. We've found with our own books that the more we educate people about the world of internet marketing and online customer attraction, the more they appreciate the value that a really good company can bring them. Not only does it position us well, but it also clearly shows the high value of good quality marketing.

Let's look at an example relating to consultancy, a market traditionally wary of 'giving away their best stuff':

Jill is a business consultant and she wants to help entrepreneurs to grow their businesses through good quality marketing, hiring the right people and planning for growth. She decides to try and get down everything she knows and put it into a book to sell on Amazon. She spends a couple of months producing a fantastic book which gives entrepreneurs a really useful set of exercises and tools to grow their business. She includes plenty of case studies and examples to illustrate and bring her points to life.

Imagine that you read such a book. Would your thoughts be:

1. This book is extremely useful and Jill is clearly an authority. I can only imagine the value of an ongoing coaching relationship with Jill where she can help me to implement some of the ideas in this fantastic book.
2. Jill has clearly given everything in this book. I've managed to learn and implement absolutely everything she has explained with 100% effectiveness. There would be no point working with Jill, and instead I'll go and find someone who has written a less comprehensive book to work with.

You get the point. Give your audience a fire hose to drink from. Allow them to get some early results themselves that prove the effectiveness of what you're teaching, then drive them to an offer on your website to take the relationship a step further.

At the time of writing I'm also working on a guide for self publishing and promoting your first book, which will be released in early 2014. Sign up for the free updates to this book at http://exposureninja.com/101 to be the first to get access to the new book when it is released/.

Be the Expert in your industry

The horse that wins the race by a nose takes the lion's share of the prize money, despite only winning by a nose. A-list movie stars command a multiple of the fee that lesser-known stars attract, despite working the same hours. Nature is not linear in this regard. In the same way, the most high profile businesses in a market take a disproportionate share. This applies on a local level just as much as for national and international companies.

But what makes a business high-profile, and how can businesses *raise* their profiles in order to attract a larger share of the pie? A short example illustrates how most business owners focus entirely in the wrong area.

Coming from the musician world, I grew up with the belief that practice was directly proportional to success.

"How do you get to Carnegie Hall?" the lost tourists asked the busker on a street corner a few blocks away. "Practice, practice, practice"

It's a cute joke, and the mindset sells a lot of tutorial books and lessons. But the principle is completely and totally wrong. The world is full of geniuses sharpening their saws in the dark, totally unknown and broke.

But being the expert is about more than just *knowing your stuff*.

For every Jamie Oliver, Gordon Ramsay or any other TV chef, there are thousands of 'real' chefs complaining that they should be the famous ones because they are more skilled at food preparation. They spend hours in the kitchen perfecting their dishes, experimenting with different ways to prepare ingredients and being truly innovative. They are all about the food rather than chasing celebrity, so believe that they deserve the exposure. Yet it's the TV chefs who have the fat bank accounts and whose names sell many more meals in their restaurants.

And yes, for every hopeless singer on X Factor there are thousands of frustrated genius musicians practicing 9 hours a day and *completely missing the point*.

Being the expert or authority is only half about knowing your stuff. Competence is important, but it's not where the real riches are. The other half is about being *seen* to know your stuff by a lot of people. The key is the "a lot of people" bit, as visibility is absolutely fundamental to the authority piece. It's about cultivating yourself as a celebrity. Not the Paris Hilton kind (although there is a book worth of lessons there!) but a celebrity in the sense that you become recognisable *in your market, with your target audience*.

Cultivating your expert status online

How do you promote this expert status throughout your online marketing?

The answer is that it's built into everything that you do. From your website copy to your social media; your guest posts and magazine articles to your book. Everywhere that you have a platform, seek to educate and help your audience. You want them to crave every piece of content that comes from you because it's so valuable, and dripping with authority. It's about building in testimonials, stories and case studies every time you open your mouth or put your fingers to the keys.

It's also about having the confidence to proclaim your expertise and be willing to take your place on the podium. While this can seem intimidating to those who have spent their lives trying to fit in and remain invisible, it's surprising how easy it is to adapt once you begin to see the results of this approach.

Cultivating expert status should be a main priority for business owners that want to build highly visible businesses. It's time to leave behind the comfort of anonymity and proclaim your arrival. Write your book, share your knowledge, build that email list, and don't let anyone - including yourself - stop you from snatching the 'expert' crown, snapping a selfie, and posting it slap bang in the centre of your market.

If you haven't already done so, head over to http://exposureninja.com/101 to receive free lifetime updates to this book, as well as a completely free 7 Point Online Marketing Review worth £186. Our team will help you create a customised strategic plan to boost your image and credibility in your market, and can work with you to implement it, if required.

Your Website

For most businesses, their website is their most important marketing asset. And yet most businesses are making a few key mistakes on their website which severely limits the flow of new customers from the Internet. Your website is like your shop front, your shop interior and your shop brochure all rolled into one. Further, nothing is neutral. If it's not representing you well, then it's damaging your reputation (and your business).

In the age of social media, Adwords and Google it can be all to easy to become distracted by anything other than the big fat elephant sat in the middle of it all: your site.

It's the centre of everything online, and will remain the centre for the near future. So in 2014, making sure your website is representing you well and converting visitors to customers, should be top priority.

In this section we'll go through our top Website tips to make your business more money using your website. These are distilled from years of experience working with successful and unsuccessful business websites, testing, measuring and experimenting.

Hopefully you'll find a lot of common sense here, although you might have noticed that a lot of websites opt for a 'common sense bypass'. When you're find a common sense tip, may we humbly suggest that you revisit your site through the eyes of Homer Simpson and just make 100% sure that you're in compliance before moving on.

Many of the business owners whose sites we review are surprised just how unclear their sites are to those who aren't already familiar with their business. Pitching your site at a Homer Simpson level is about right for most internet users. Not because they're dumb, but because they are busy, distracted and unfamiliar. We as business owners are so involved in our businesses that everything seems obvious to us.
With that said, let's dive straight in.

Clearly state the benefits of your business on your homepage

The exact statistics vary according to who you ask, but they all demonstrate the same pattern: your website doesn't have very long to grab your visitor's attention before they decide to stay or leave.

So how can you stack the odds in your favour and encourage visitors not only to stay, but convert?

One of the most important jobs of your website's homepage is to communicate quickly, effectively and without any confusion why visitors should do business with you. With almost infinite choice online, there is no time to mess around. Think of it as an elevator pitch, but for a single storey elevator.

Your key benefit statement sums up exactly what you do - or rather the *main benefit* of what you do - in a single sentence. The perfect benefit statement identifies who your customer is and what you do for them in a way that they can understand the value of.

Exposure Ninja's key benefit statement is 'We help businesses attract more customers from the Internet'. We don't call ourselves a 'digital agency' because that's not what our clients care about. Nobody wakes up with sudden urge to hire a digital agency, they wake up with the urge to *get more customers*. Our clients don't really care about creativity, statistics, location, history & background - other than how they affect our ability to get them more customers from the Internet, of course. Everything on the site is directed at demonstrating our ability to get them more customers from the Internet.

What sentence best describes what your business does, and how can you stick this right up front on your website to immediately tell your visitors why they should buy from you?

"Australia's favourite fancy dress store"
"The best cupcakes in the West of England"
"Effective hypnotherapy treatments to stop smoking for good"
"Finding buyers for luxury homes in San Diego"

Don't leave your visitors guessing or hunting around to see if you're right for them. Tell them straight up front: here's what we can do for you. Be fancy and clever with your design, by all means. But the key benefit statement should hit your target customer like a brick straight between the eyes: "POW this is right for me".

Use a strong call to action on every content page of your site

On every website there are two types of pages. Content pages, as the name suggests, contain the 'meat' of your website. They're the pages about the products and services you offer, the case studies, blog posts and everything that relates to your core expertise. The Extras pages contain everything else: contact details, meet the team, about us and the boring legal bits.

Each of your content pages is a potential landing page for visitors as these pages are the ones most likely to rank on Google or get shared by website visitors. Because they can be the first pages your visitors see they could also be the *last*, depending on their ability to engage your audience. So not only does each of your content pages need to clearly state your mission and benefits, but it also needs to drive visitors to take the next step in their relationship with you, whilst preventing them from clicking away.

Whether the goal for your website is to attract enquiries through a form, generate phone calls, emails, or trigger direct purchases, this desired action should be possible from every relevant content page. At the very least, your desired action should be only one (extremely obvious) click away. With very few exceptions, hiding away calls to action or requiring people to hunt for the Contact page in order to get in touch is an unprofitable move, because each time you require your visitors to take a desired action, you'll lose some of them. If it takes 3 clicks for them to reach the desired outcome, most will have disappeared long ago.

Make it simple and tell your visitors exactly what they need to do to move to the next stage of their relationship with you. Do this on every page of your site and it won't matter how your audience finds you or where they end up.

Using Bait in your lead capture

No matter how appealing your website is, how tantalizing your offers are and how good your benefit statements, there will always be a certain number of visitors who just aren't ready to buy from you yet. If the only call to action on your website is 'buy now' or even 'get in touch', then you're isolating all those who just aren't ready or willing to take that action yet.

The solution is to offer some attractive bait in return for their contact details. The simplest example we can use to illustrate is our very own online marketing review. Not every visitor to Exposure Ninja's website is ready to buy a new website, SEO, Pay per click management or social media marketing. So we offer something of high value (expert analysis of their website and online marketing) for no charge. This then allows us to start building a relationship with each prospect. Not only do they receive the review and customised action plan, but they also receive emails from us in future offering discounts on new books, information about Google updates and other information designed to help them in their goal to attract more business from the Internet. When the time comes to buy a new website or step up their online marketing, we already have a relationship and are *far* more likely to get the business. But it all starts with a form asking for a name and email address.

Lead capture works in every business - we haven't found one that it doesn't work in yet. From dentists offering $15 checkups or free teeth whitening, bands offering a free taster EP, plumbers offering a discounted boiler servicing and accountants offering free phone consultations... there's *always* an appealing angle that you can use to attract potential customers.

Historically the 'free report' has been the bait of choice for many in this situation. But with customers more savvy than ever, reports don't hold the perceived value they once did. As a rule, you want to give away enough to whet the appetite of your audience and get their greed glands secreting, without attracting unqualified freeloaders. Your bait should also demonstrate the core benefits of your offering, whether it's quality, expertise, reliability, or appearance. It should increase the likelihood of the sale considerably, and in many cases it can actually be the first step of the sale.

When deciding on your bait, Clearly each business has to take into consideration not only their profit for each new customer (a luxury yacht company can give away juicier bait than a company manufacturing earphones, for example) but also the number of leads they expect to attract, to make sure that their bait is scalable.

Be aware and take care of Researchers, Comparers and Red Hots

There are 3 basic levels of valuable website visitors:
1. Interested researchers
2. Comparers
3. Red Hots

The Interested Researchers are not ready to buy yet. They are looking to see if what you offer will satisfy their need, fit their approximate price range and help them move closer towards their goals.

The Comparers are a step further along. They already know that what you offer will suit them and they're at the stage of comparing different options to find the most suitable one for them. People in the comparison stage are unlikely to buy before they decide exactly which option is most suitable for them. At this point, they become a Red Hot.

Red Hots are ready to go. They've got their credit card in hand and they're looking for somewhere to plug it in. Depending on the size of the purchase, red hots might still need some reassurance from you before deciding to do business, but they're sold on buying *something* now or very soon, and it's your job to convert them.

You'll notice that only one of these 3 categories of website visitor is actually in a buying mood. The Red Hots are also generally the smallest group, and yet most of our websites are geared towards satisfying them and extracting their business. The Interested Researchers and Comparers are ignored, but not lost. Just because they're not ready to buy now, this doesn't mean they never will. The beauty of the three tiers is that over time, we can move people up through the tiers to become Red Hots and then on to buyers.

Target lead generation and CTAs at different levels

Of all the three groups of visitors to your site (Researchers, Comparers and Red Hots), only one puts money on your bottom line *today*: the Red Hots. So it's your goal to move as many visitors as possible into the Red Hot category.

To do this, you need to make sure that you have elements on your website which attract and satisfy Researchers and Comparers as well, so that you can pick them up and help them move along the interest line.

Interested Researchers like information. Case studies, testimonials, descriptions, specifications, videos - the more research material you can provide, the more you'll satisfy the researchers.

The Comparers have a desire for information which, although on the surface it appears similar to the researchers, is much deeper and demonstrates higher commercial intent. They want to understand the relative benefits of different offerings, the additional features of your service, your guarantees and anything else that differentiates you from your competitors.

While these groups aren't ready to 'Click to buy' or 'Call us Now', they *are* ideal targets of a lead capture campaign. Targeting your Interested Researchers and Comparers with a piece of juicy bait and collecting their contact details allows you to continue to groom them over time, providing them with the information they need to move up the ladder. When they're ready to become Red Hots, they'll already be familiar with your offering and you'll be at the front of their mind.

The call to action on your website that you use to attract IRs and Comparers needs to be softer than a 'Buy Now' or 'Call us Now'. Remember that your goal is to build a relationship over time and the first step is to trade something of value for your visitor's contact details. An appealing bait for a Researcher or Comparer might be a document about future trends in your market, a free sample or some case studies showing use of your products or services in the real world. Whatever bait you choose, it should satisfy two main criteria:

1. It should be of high enough perceived value that your visitors are eager to trade it for their contact details.
2. It should move them closer to buying with you. Demonstrating the core benefit of your product or service is a good way to do this as it simultaneously satisfies their research and/or comparison desires, thus allowing them to move towards the buying decision.

Commit to including elements on your site to entice the IRs and Comparers, and capture their contact details. Set up an email list for them and build an automated email campaign to move them up the buying ladder. Once you've taken responsibility for farming your own prospects, you'll have the confidence knowing that potential customers are constantly moving up and becoming ready to buy.

Write a profitable blog

Huh? Yes, your blog can make you money.

A profitable blog for your business is one that becomes a destination for people in your industry to find out about the latest news and get your take on things. Positioning yourself as an expert is a very good way to attract high quality customers, and your blog is one of the most powerful authority-building tools you have at your disposal.

Most blogs are dry and totally uninteresting. 'New Website Launched' epitomises the poorly planned blog post, simultaneously demonstrating both the writer's complete self centredness with their lack of discipline as it sits atop the 'recent posts' widget, despite being 9 months old. Just try to hold back the hordes of rabid customers desperate to share this vital information with their friends and colleagues: "Did you see? Boredom & Co have a new WEBSITE!"

The smart business owner uses their blog as they would a seminar, conference talk or interview: to demonstrate their expertise, give their audience useful information that moves them closer towards their goals, and of course mention any relevant products or services that can make this happen faster.

Comment on latest news but make sure to give your opinion and add value. What does this news *mean* for your audience? How can your readers take advantage? What's the wider trend here and how can they position themselves ready to capitalise on it? If you give away your best information on your blog, you'll never have to worry about attracting readers, social shares or any of the other things that most dull blog writers have long given up on.

The ideal blog post length and depth varies according to your readership and positioning. Seth Godin's posts are short and sweet, which suits his audience and the fact that he's really not making any specialist recommendations at all - just general observations. Meanwhile the technical company sharing their latest test results or predicting future trends will probably find a long-form post works better for them. Their audience of technical specialists will treat a longer post with more credibility and it gives an opportunity to share all the research and statistics necessary to present a convincing case.

The same consumption rules apply to blogs as any other online content. Use headlines and subheadlines to break up the text and clearly define each section, and help those of us with shorter attention span to find the content that we're most interested in. Pictures and illustrations can and should be used to create interest and split up long sections of text which can be quite intimidating on a screen.

Remember that you don't have to be the only one contributing to the blog. If some of your team have specialist knowledge and feel enthusiastic about it, trusting them to create some blog posts can take the pressure off you and help to fill the gaps between your own posts.

Of course the posts themselves are only one part of running a profitable blog. They need to be adequately promoted across your website and through your social media channels. Include social share buttons on the blog and with each blog post to make it really simple for readers to share content they find interesting or useful.

You can also use Facebook Comments on your blog posts rather than your platform's commenting system. The advantage here is that when your readers comment on your posts, they're automatically sharing that content on Facebook, making it visible to their friends.

Your blog pages themselves should have all of the key elements that any other pages on your site have, for example calls to action, contact details or forms and benefit statements. Any new visitor to your blog should be able to tell immediately what it is that you do, why that's relevant to them and what they need to do next if they're interested in your product or service.

Lastly, if you've got a plan for your blog make sure that you see it through. Rome wasn't built in a day and neither are high-traffic, profitable blogs. You're going to have to spend some time making posts that aren't immediately popular while you're building up your audience, and there's really no shortcut to this. So don't be disheartened if your blog doesn't appear to get many readers for the first few months. Stick at it and you'll find your audience growing steadily.

The Power of a Good Headline

A good headline can transform the effectiveness of any web page, ad or post because a good headline gets content read. Headlines act like an advert grabbing the reader, sitting them down and shoving your page or post under their noses. The best headlines put your audience in the right frame of mind and condition them to be receptive to your message as well. Compare the following two headlines:

Headline 1: The shocking and barely legal way to spy on your employees that turbocharges productivity by 72%

Headline 2: New activity monitoring software beta launches on Wednesday in San Francisco

I defy anyone running a team not to click on headline 1, whereas headline 2 is of little interest to anyone other than other activity monitoring software companies. Both headlines are promoting the same thing, but obviously headline 1 focusses on what the potential customers would be most interested in (increasing productivity) and uses intrigue ('barely legal', 'spy'). Meanwhile the second headline sounds like it was written by the accountant, and has about as much sizzle as the 1-times table.

The best places to study effective headline writing is on the lowest common denominator newspaper websites. In the UK we have the Daily Mail website, which is an absolute headline goldmine and can keep a visitor of almost any demographic 'busy' for at least 5 minutes. In the US, the National Enquirer offers a similar excellent quality of headline to compensate for the low quality journalism. Incidentally, because these publications thrive or die on the strength of their headlines, the folks writing these headlines are some of the highest paid writers in the world.

So there's the excuse you need to use next time you're caught 'studying' sensationalist trash during work hours.

You might be thinking *"but my business has an image to maintain and that sort of headline doesn't reflect the sort of message we want to portray."*

We hear you, honestly. Each time you write an ad, blog post, status update or email you have a choice: create a headline designed to entice, intrigue and capture, or play it completely straight. How far along the line you decide to go is your call, and it's not our place to try and convince you one way or the other.

But whatever you do, please resist the temptation to think that your demographic is too sophisticated to fall for 'hype'. This book could just as easily have been called 'Internet marketing observations for businesses', but you probably wouldn't have bought it. No one likes to think of themselves as gullible or susceptible to this sort of advertising, but the fact remains that, as humans, we all obey the same basic urges. That's why the smartest and most successful marketers on the planet use this type of shortcuts to get the results they do.

Answer your customer's top 3 questions immediately

Every person that visits your website has 3 questions at the front of their mind. If you can answer all 3 quickly and satisfactorily, you've bought enough time to persuade them to stay and have a look around. Fail the three question test, and you're out.

The three questions are:
1. What is this website about?
2. Can it help me to get to where I want to be? (What's in it for me?)
3. Can I trust it?

Questions 1 and 2 are addressed through the content, primarily on your homepage, and 1 or 2 clicks deep *if you're lucky*. You have no time to waste in being specific about who you are and what you do (question one), and this information should be presented in a way that answers question 2.

Question 3 is usually subconscious and a lot more complex to analyse. It is made up of a number of different factors, from page loading speed (slow can indicate 'broken') to the look and layout of the pages (homemade or amateurish can indicate a less established or unsuccessful business). Of course visible Trustpilot reviews, verified payment logos and customer testimonials can help to build trust on a conscious level, but visitors still won't buy from a site that 'doesn't feel right'.

A good question to help identify this problem is, "were this site new to you, would you be comfortable putting in your credit card information?" Whether or not you actually accept payment through your site doesn't matter, this level of trust should be the minimum that you aim for, and until you can answer an honest 'yes' work needs to be done.

Use the right text on your homepage

If your website's purpose is to generate customers, the text on your homepage tells customers (and Google) who you are, what you do and why people should use you rather than your competitors. It is not the best place for elaborate corporate-y mission statements, and neither is it the place to *only* show some fancy-looking pictures. Yes, you should include pictures on your homepage - preferably big ones if your product or service looks good - but it's not the pictures that will make people buy, it's the text.

The text on your homepage should tell your audience what you do or what you are, *in their language*. From an SEO perspective, you want to include the exact words and phrases that your customers search for to find you, so that Google can confidently show your website high in the search results for these phrases. From a marketing and psychology perspective, the presence of the exact phrases your customers use serves to show them immediately that they've found what they were looking for.

It sounds so basic but you'd be amazed how few sites get this right. Here's the quick check that we run with business owners who want to know how well-optimised their front pages are:

Pick one phrase that you would like to rank top of Google for. It might be the description of your business ("beauty school") or a product or service that you sell, which you know customers search for ("makeup courses"). Visit your homepage and do a search for that phrase. If you're really feeling brave try the same thing with a second target phrase, third phrase and so on. How did you do? Here's a rough scoring guide:

- Excellent: Your main target phrase appears in the main headline on your homepage and is immediately visible to visitors. It also appears at least twice more on your homepage in the body text or in sub headlines. Your second and third phrases appear in subheadlines and also in the body text.
- Good: Your main target phrase appears multiple times on your homepage with at least one of these instances being a headline or sub headline. Your second phrase appears at least once.
- Average: Your main target phrase appears at least once on your homepage. Second and third phrases don't appear, and usually for sites in the average category the process of identifying the second and third phrase was quite difficult.
- Poor: The words in your main target phrase appear on your homepage, although not as a complete phrase. There are less than 100 words in total in the homepage.
- Catastrophic: The words in your main target phrase do not appear on your homepage at all, or there is very little text on your homepage. The site will be incredibly unlikely to rank well and unlikely to bring you much (if any) business.

If your score was lower than you'd like, it's time to get excited. This tip is one of those we call 'low hanging fruit' because it's like your website has been driving with the handbrake on. Make it a priority to get this sorted immediately, as once you address this you should see an improvement in ranking *even if nothing else is changed*.

Organise the information on your site in a clear and logical way

Both from a user and SEO standpoint, how you structure the information about your business on your website is really important. Your website's structure and navigation should be such that visitors can find the information they need within 1 or 2 page loads at most.

It's a good idea to break your information down into clearly defined pages targeted to each topic. It's probably easiest to look at an example to illustrate:

David runs a small accountancy firm based in Manchester, UK, mainly serving small businesses. David's typical work is tax returns, VAT (tax) returns, payroll and advising his clients on how to grow their businesses. He notices that most of his competitors online have a single 'Services' page on their website which lists all of the services they offer. But he decides that this is suboptimal because it means that anyone looking to see if they offer VAT returns has to trawl through a lot of content not relevant to them just to find out.

He decides to instead have a number of different pages under the Services heading, each targeted to a specific customer or service. His website structure ends up looking something like this:

- Home
- Accountancy Services
  - Tax returns
  - Payroll
  - VAT returns
  - Tax advice
  - Company formation
- Testimonials
- Free Consultation
- Contact Us

All of the pages under the Accountancy Services page are reachable by a drop down menu, so visitors can navigate to them with one click from anywhere on the site. The structure is logical and it's easy for potential clients to find the information they need without having to dig around.

Each of his service pages talks in detail about the particular service, his business's typical clients and gives some example case studies. Each page has a call to action offering a free consultation session to discuss how suitable the service would be for the client. Of course there's the standard business information such as address, areas they serve and contact details as well.

By structuring the website in this way, each of the service pages (provided that they are optimised effectively) are far more likely to rank well for phrases like "Small business payroll accountant Manchester" or "VAT returns Manchester". Were all this information rolled into one page, it would be far less likely to have an impact on the search results.

Take into consideration what's 'above the fold'

One of the killer mistakes that geeks make when designing websites on their huge 27" monitor screens is only making the sites look great on 27" monitor screens. By far the most common monitor size is 15" and your site needs to perform just as effectively on smaller screens as it does on huge cinema-like displays.

One of the main considerations in web design is what to show 'above the fold' - the section of the screen that is visible without scrolling down. While it's inaccurate to think of site visitors as brain dead morons completely unable to scroll a mouse down a page, it's good practice not to make them hunt around *too* much to find your main call to action or most important message. We tend to favour placing lead capture elements above the fold wherever possible, for example, because visitors spot them immediately and by placing them high up you can emphasise their importance.

There's a really useful website that will show you how much of your site is visible above the fold on different screen sizes: http://www.whereisthefold.com/

Optimise your website for mobile

Mobile device use is growing faster than anybody anticipated, and with around 40% of searches now happening on mobile devices, making sure your website looks good and works well on mobile is no longer an optional extra.

Optimising for mobile is about making sure that visitors on phones and tablets see a version of your site that is easy to navigate, read and interact with. The problem with viewing regular websites on smaller screens is that the text is tiny and viewers need to zoom in and out to find their way around the page. Clicking links and menu items is a nightmare, and the whole experience increases the likelihood of missing the sale.

You have two choices when it comes to serving mobile customers: a separate mobile website, or making your existing website *responsive* to the size of the viewing screen.

Mobile Website

A mobile site is an entirely separate site that is automatically served to visitors using a small screen. This mobile site can thus be optimised for mobile use by using big buttons easy to click with big fat fingers, concise text and navigation that comes down rather than across the page. The layout of the mobile site will usually be significantly different to the desktop site, placing the elements on the page in order of importance to mobile viewers, and fitting on the narrower screen.

The advantage of mobile websites is this flexibility to build a layout suited to mobile, independent of the desktop version.

The disadvantage is that because there are now two distinct websites, the admin and updating tasks double. Another issue is that with the range of screen sizes now available, there tends to be a blurred line between the phone and tablet screen size where a mobile site looks too small and a desktop site is too big.

Responsive Website

Responsiveness is behaviour built in to your existing website that allows it to 'respond' to the size of the viewing screen, adapting its layout to suit. This is a very neat and efficient way to present your site across screens of any size, whilst still keeping a consistent look and feel. Elements can be rearranged for smaller screens, and repositioned so as to show the most important parts at the top.

The advantage of responsive sites is that they work well on any screen size without requiring you to maintain a separate mobile site.

In most cases we recommend responsive websites to clients having a new site built, or where it is cost-effective to code in responsive behaviour. Sometimes however, a mobile site makes the most sense, particularly if the original desktop site is inaccessible or particularly complex.

What about apps?

Here's the truth about mobile apps for businesses: in the vast majority of cases, they are a complete and utter waste of time.

The good thing about apps for web marketing companies (like us) is that they have a high profit margin because clients have no idea how much work goes into creating an app. The bad news is that most of these apps rarely get downloaded and have no measurable effect on the client's business. That's why we usually advise businesses to avoid apps, and focus their attention on improving their websites.

There are exceptions (of course) when apps can work well:

- E-commerce businesses that generate frequent purchases.
- Services genuinely needed by customers out in the field, a lot.
- Businesses trying to build loyalty through a rewards or voucher scheme.

If in doubt, take a look in the app store and see if you can find apps from similar businesses. If they look dead, old fashioned and dusty, thank your lucky stars that you weren't the sucker conned into paying £5000 for each of them.

Make your website the source for new information in your industry

If you want to build up a regular readership for your blog, make it the place that your audience knows they can get the latest information about goings on in your industry. This is a strategy that requires a good amount of commitment, and you (or someone in your business) needs to invest time into scanning press releases from manufacturers, other companies and anyone else likely to be creating news.

It's also a longer-term strategy and it can take a site a year or longer to establish itself as a true authority, but if you have the man or woman power to do it and you're truly committed to building a high authority position, it's very effective.

One of the fastest ways to get your site known and bookmarked as a source of news is to build an audience of other high authority figures. Their retweets, shares and links will be valuable to your own visibility and help you to attract a still wider audience. We'll look further at building this audience through authority outreach in the Social Media section.

To make sure that you're collecting your audience effectively, use social like, share and tweet buttons and remember to offer a subscriber option so that readers can submit their email address to receive updates automatically.

A high traffic and authoritative blog is also a great place to run some lead generation offers to capitalise on the quality visitors you're attracting. You could offer an 'insider's club' where members can get the latest news and tips that non-members don't get access to, or a free report giving an overview or 101 guide to a particular topic. Over time this sort of lead generation on a blog with decent traffic can build you a large and profitable list, making you money through direct sales of your products and services, through affiliate relationships or advertising.

Collect Testimonials on your website

Testimonials are such an important sales tool and yet very few businesses use them to anything like their full extent. By positioning testimonials prominently on your website, they allow us to extol the virtues of your business in a more believable way - through the words of others.

They also counteract one of the main deficiencies of online marketing, namely the lack of personal or face-to-face experience. When people express hesitation at doing business with a company over the net, what they're really saying is that the risk of being caught out outweighs the potential reward. By boosting your credibility with copious use of testimonials you're addressing this issue head on: "look, it worked out for all of *these* people".

There are a few different ways to collect and display testimonials online, and each has its own advantages and disadvantages. Whichever you choose, remember that a poor testimonial strategy in action is infinitely more profitable than the world's best testimonial strategy that remains in the planning phase indefinitely. If you know that you won't get it done, take a shortcut to get *something* workable up in the meantime.

The testimonial strategy you choose will depend largely on the following factors:
- Your resources: time, budget.
- The size of your audience. A small consultancy and large e-commerce store have very different requirements and priorities when it comes to gathering and displaying testimonials.
- The technical aspect: implementing different review systems on your site.

DIY Review collection

The simplest way to collect and display reviews is to ask customers directly for their testimonials and simply add them onto your site in sidebars, body copy and on a *testimonials* or *case studies* page. This requires no fanciness, third parties, automated processes or plugins. The advantage of this method for smaller businesses is the simplicity and, as long as you can add the reviews to your site relatively cheaply, the cost savings.

The disadvantage of DIY review collection is that the reviews can lack a sense of being verified. The website visitor is forced to trust that what you write on the site is a legitimate review from a real customer. The more detail you can give, the more trusting you'll find your visitors are willing to be. Full names, locations, website addresses and photos are all really useful tools to back up and prove legitimacy. Nothing says 'fake review' more than a reviewer called J. Smith or, worse still, "J.S". If your reviewer is willing to be identified, go the whole nine yards.

Of course there are businesses for whom identifying customers is not desirable. An example is pest control where the clients might not be too keen for Google searches of their name to return detailed information about their rat infestation. In cases like this, the challenge is to be specific about *something*. It could be the specifics of their requirements or their vital stats. The more detail you can give, the more legitimacy the review holds. Let's look at the pest control example:

Tim's Pest Control serves domestic and commercial customers around Garland, Texas. The trouble is that none of our clients want to have their pest issues publicised, but Tim *really* wants to include prominent detailed testimonials on his website because he knows what this will do for his business. So he decides to be specific about what he can be specific about, whilst leaving out the parts that will explicitly identify the customer:

"Wow! Tim and the team fixed our cockroach infestation literally overnight. I've never seen someone eat so many. It was no hassle, they arrived very discretely in unmarked vehicles and importantly there was no mess or cleaning up. The work was done over the weekend, avoiding disruption to office hours" - Medical supplies business owner in Garland, TX. Office building downtown, approximately 4000 sq ft. Cockroaches had spread throughout the office, kitchen area and into the ceiling.

Notice how much more credibility this review has than one signed simply "JM" or even signed nothing at all? By giving more detail about the customer's problem and the work carried out, the solution immediately gains credibility with others in a similar situation: "My office is approximately 4000sq feet, what a good fit" or "our cockroach infestation sounds similar".

So in order to boost credibility of DIY testimonials that you have gathered and published yourself, use as much detail as you possibly can. In this sense, we're starting to move towards case studies:

Testimonials deluxe: Case Studies

If your business deals with relatively few customers or offers a very tailored service, in addition to testimonials you might want to consider running a case studies page on your website. Through case studies you can dive deeper into the story behind a particular result or interaction with a customer. Just as with detailed testimonials, case studies allow potential customers to see connections between *their* situation and the situations in the case studies. This builds affinity (*this is for me*), social proof (*I'm making a popular choice*) as well as demonstrating the effectiveness of your product or service.

Running a case studies page is an absolute no brainer for any business involved in consultancy or offering a personalised service, whether B2B or B2C. Wedding dress shops, estate agencies, car dealers... if your business relies on an element of personal service, you should be shouting from the rooftops with the stories of successful past customer experiences.

Automatic testimonial collection

Taking a step up in complexity from the DIY testimonial collection is using a form on your website to allow customers to upload their own testimonials. Not only does this free up your time from having to manually add the testimonials (which it's very easy to procrastinate on), but if it's worked properly it can also boost their credibility.

The key is to make the testimonial submission and display area very clearly linked. Website visitors that see a testimonial submission form and believe that submitting a testimonial (good or bad) will make it show up in the testimonial display area are more likely to believe the testimonials that they see are real. It looks natural and less susceptible to tampering or falsification: *I believe that the testimonials shown on this page were supplied by people entering their details into this form.*

We implement this sort of testimonial system on many of our client's sites, including through our tradesmen website business. Tradesmen are not a business category well known for their use of testimonials so this has been a very interesting experience. The reality is that anyone searching for a gas engineer will be able to view the websites of 10-20 gas engineers on the front page of Google and, in many areas, they won't see a single testimonial on any of them. We realised early on that there is a reason for this and that the tradesmen themselves were unlikely to collect and send us reviews for manual inclusion on the website. We needed to be more elegant in our approach and avoid the tradesmen themselves whenever possible.

So we started integrating a system to collect reviews on their sites which would then display them in the Google-readable hReview format. Because the sites were built in Wordpress, we used the Customer Reviews plugin which takes care of this all automatically, and also has a handy review approval system that allows you to filter out or address negative reviews.

The next step was building this into a system that required as close to zero effort for the tradesmen. We needed to get their customers to review them on their website in order to help them generate more work, but relying on the tradesman him or herself to ask the customers to do this was about as much use as standing on the coast of Ireland trying to shout to America. Very exhausting and utterly futile.

So we printed business cards for each tradesman to give to their customers once the job was finished. It had their contact details on so they'd be easily reachable for any future work - by itself a marketing revolution for many of these folks. But on the back of the cards, we gave instructions for how to leave a review on the tradesman's new website. We made it simple for customers to do, and they responded. Of course, not all of the tradesmen actually give out their cards, but those that do collect vastly more testimonials and, as a result, their websites bring in more work for them. We learnt from this the importance of implementing a *review collection system*, rather than just periodically trying to collect some reviews.

Third Party review services

There are a number of companies trying to improve the trustworthiness of Internet reviews. Trustpilot and Feefo are two examples of third party sites whose sole purpose is to collect and publish reviews of businesses. They seek to make it as seamless as possible for the business owner by emailing past customers on your behalf, asking for reviews and then verifying the reviews for you.

The benefit of using one of these types of services is that they can give you an extra level of credibility. By displaying the Trustpilot or Feefo widget on your site, visitors can immediately see a trustworthiness score. Of course this relies on your audience being savvy enough to understand what Trustpilot, Feefo or any of the others actually do. If they have no idea, then the displayed reviews are likely to hold less weight.

Services like these also submit their ratings to Google, allowing a seller rating to show up in Adwords ads, for example. In our testing we've seen a significant boost in Click Through Rate when these seller ratings are used. Increasing Click Through Rate also tends to decrease cost per click, ultimately saving money on ad traffic.

The disadvantage of these services is the cost. Trustpilot in the UK starts at £75 per month which, depending on your traffic volume, could be far more profitably invested elsewhere in online marketing.

However you decide to go about collecting and displaying reviews on your website and across your online marketing, the most important thing is to just get started. You can always adjust course later on. And remember that 5 testimonials are better than 4, 10 are better than 9 and 392 are better than 391. Don't stop just because you think you've collected enough: you never know which one will push that 'on the edge' customer over the line.

Use your testimonials to do your selling for you

Now that you've got some ideas for collecting and displaying your testimonials, let's think about how you can use them to do your selling work for you.

As mentioned above, testimonials are a socially acceptable way for you to say very nice things about your business. If I were to say "Exposure Ninja is probably the best advertising and marketing investment for small and medium sized companies anywhere on the planet", a percentage of readers would take me seriously. But most would treat it with a healthy dose of scepticism and assume that it was marketing 'puffery'.

It's very different hearing people *outside* the business talk about the virtues of a product or service, and it holds much more weight. Social proof is an efficient decision making shortcut and using testimonials in your sales copy allows you to take full advantage of it.

If I were to say to a potential client, "one of our clients in a similar field to yours earned a return on investment of

15 times (not an increase of 15%, 15 *times*), in one week, last Christmas and told us *'I'll be honest with you, it's the best money I've ever spent'"* that holds much more weight than any opinion I can present. The words "It's the best money I've ever spent" speak straight to the customer in that moment of decision when they're trying to weigh up whether or not to make the investment in their business.

There are two ways that you can use testimonials on your website and in your marketing materials, and of course you can combine both:

1. By using quotes throughout, illustrating your main points. For example using blockquotes or annotations in the text. If you're talking about the quality of your personal service, a good testimonial saying how good your service was underlines this point and gives more weight to your statement.

2. More covert use through illustrative stories. Throughout this and our other books, there are dozens of stories about businesses that we've helped to grow and attract more customers through the Internet. They are useful tools to illustrate and inspire, but they also help to position us in a way that demonstrates our results without us talking about how good we think we are. This type of covert case study use should not be overlooked and there are very few businesses who *can't* use this strategy to boost sales. Stories of this sort work well in 'free

information guides' sent out to potential customers.

Testimonials shown prominently on your website should emphasise your main selling points. Again, let them do the talking for you where possible. Two prominent testimonials talking about the excellent service your customers received from you, immediately set up an expectation in potential visitor's mind that excellent service is part of your offering. It doesn't need to be stated any more explicitly than that.

Use landing pages to track campaigns

Profitable marketing is all about tracking and measuring, and thanks to analytics, trackable numbers and email capture forms, there's really no excuse for not knowing the return on each of your campaigns.

Landing pages are a useful tracking tool, particularly when you're driving visitors to your website from offline, or without a trackable click. An example when this is useful is when tracking leads from magazine articles. If a number of different articles are running at the same time, driving readers of each magazine to the same page on your website makes it difficult to track which magazines are most effective at bringing in leads. But by sending each magazine's leads to a different landing page (for example www.exposureninja.com/landing1, www.exposureninja.com/landing2) you can more accurately track how many leads and conversions each title brings you.

Let's take an example for a high end Hi Fi consultancy company. They have articles placed in a number of high-end home and design magazines, whose readers would be ideal customers. For each article, they offer the same lead generation bait: a free guide to Hi Fi installation trends in 2014. This is intended to appeal to those interested in the latest Hi Fi technology who are thinking about buying in the New Year. The articles themselves give an overview of the trends, then the call to action paragraph at the end drives readers to a landing page where they can download the full trend report.

Each landing page has a lead capture form on, but these forms are not connected to the same email list. So that each magazine's audience gets a tailored experience, the lists are split into different magazines so that the communication can refer to the magazine the reader originally read about the business in. The landing pages themselves can be tailored to match the magazine, which will increase their conversion rate. But the most important advantage is that you, the marketer, knows exactly which magazine generated the most leads. If you decide to run ad campaigns in the future, you have some useful data about the sort of numbers that you might expect from each magazine, based on the type of offer you made. This allows you to make educated and rational decisions when it comes to ad budget.

Of course landing pages are not restricted to offline media such as magazines and flyers, and should be used in Adwords campaigns, guest blogging, social media advertising and any time you want to give people a specific message (usually an offer or lead generation bait).

Give your visitors what they want within 2 page loads (maximum)

One of the largest and most fatal nails in the coffin for many sites is poorly thought out navigation. With drop down menus and access to in-page analytics showing you exactly where people are clicking and which content is most popular, there really is absolutely no excuse for confusing visitors or burying content deep where they can't find it.

The rule we obey for all our own and client sites is that whatever people are looking for, they should be able to find it within 2 page loads at an absolute maximum. Examples of successful navigation within 2 pages loads are:

- Users are greeted by a form on the front page. They fill in the form to see search results (one page load) and click on search result for their info (second page load). Job search websites and E-commerce stores tend to work like this.

- Visitors to Amazon are shown category drop down menu, through which they can find a category of interest and click to see the bestsellers in that category (one page load). They can then browse the bestsellers and click on a product to find out more information about it and buy (second page load).
- Gmail or hotmail users wanting to check their email first sign in (one page load) then click the email to read it (second page load).
- Using Google we type in our search and hit return (one page load) before choosing from the list of search results and clicking our choice (second page load).

It's interesting to note that all of the above are structured to minimise the barriers (actions and page loads) between users and the information they seek. Online banking, on the other hand, is typically much more laborious. It's quite common for there to be 4 page loads before the balance is shown, and there will often be additional interruptive page loads for notifications (usually irrelevant or annoying for the user) or 'security' measures. Consequently, many people's impression of Internet banking is that it's slow, frustrating and behind the times. The space is certainly ripe for innovation, from a web usability perspective at least.

When visiting a new site for the first time, people tend to get frustrated after 2 page loads if they're not within sight of their goal. At three page loads we start to assume that the site doesn't contain the information we're looking for. It's instructive to notice how short our patience is when it comes to navigation. Imagine your users with 10 tabs open, ready to switch to one of your competitors should they have trouble finding what they're looking for in an acceptable time frame for them.

Increase the speed of your site to improve rankings and conversions

Website speed is not often talked about because it's a little bit technical and there's not usually much the business owner can do themselves other than demand from the tech team that they speed the website up. But it's just too important to ignore. The speed of your website has real, measurable effects on how profitable it is for you.

Mobile site speed

According to Google's Maile Ohye, the impact of a website taking an extra 1 second to load on a smartphone was a drop in page views of 9.4%. That's nearly 10% fewer pages being viewed on your site for just a 1 second increase. But it also hurts profit: the same additional second caused a 3.4% reduction in conversions. Internet users are impatient, and on mobile this impatience gets ramped up significantly.

Human Response Times: The 3 Important Limits

Jakob Neilsen's book *Usability Engineering* defines three time limits to be taken into consideration for all computer applications. Despite the fact that the book was published in 1993, the figures still hold true as we have not evolved significantly in 20 years.

- 0.1 second is the threshold for website users to feel that the site or application is responding to them in real time
- 1 second is the limit for the user's thought flow to stay uninterrupted. They'll notice the delay, but they'll approximately be in the same place they were when you left them.
- 10 seconds is the limit for keeping their attention. Thoughts will have wondered or they might start doing other things, so for delays as long or longer than 10 seconds we need to provide visual feedback to let them know when the site will be loaded.

So as you can see, 1 second page loading is the target to aim for so that we're keeping maximum engagement with the site.

Kissmetrics

According to a Kissmetrics study, 47% of web users expect a page to load within 2 seconds, and 40% of people abandon a site that takes longer than 3 seconds to load. They also claim that an additional second of loading hurts conversion rate by 7%. For an ecommerce store making $1,000 in sales each day, this 1 second will cost $25,000 each year.

Measuring your website's performance

There are a variety of free tools online to help you measure and diagnose any website speed issues you might have. The two we recommend most often are Google's PageSpeed Insights (http://developers.google.com/speed/pagespeed/insights/) which highlights any potential issues and suggests solutions, and the Web Page Test (http://www.webpagetest.org/) which gives a 'waterfall' breakdown showing how long your site takes to load, and which elements are responsible for the delays.

While detailed technical instructions for speeding up every part of your site are beyond the scope of this book, here is our list of the most common problem areas:

- Leverage Browser Caching. Your website is made up of lots of different files, including images, CSS, HTML and Javascript files. Not all of these files need to be downloaded every time someone revisits your site because many are unlikely to change from one day to the next. So to save time and bandwidth, browsers cache these files. Through your site's settings, you tell the browsers how often they need to 'refresh' these files, and obviously the longer the period between refreshes, the fewer downloads are required and the faster the page will reload. For Wordpress users, we recommend installing W3 Total Cache which handles this automatically.

- Reduce Server Response Time. This indicates how long the server takes to respond to the request for the files. If the server is slow, the site is slow to load. Low budget hosting can be a cause of long response times, particularly if you're on a shared hosting plan.
- Optimise Images. Image files can usually be compressed without losing quality, and this means shorter download times. Wordpress users can use EWWW Image Optimizer to automatically optimise the images on their site.
- Prioritise visible content. If your website loads visible content first, this gives the illusion that the site has loaded quickly. By prioritising content that appears 'above the fold', you're giving your visitors a better experience and keeping them engaged. Again, the solution to this is quite technical but Google's Page Speed Service (currently invite only, apply at https://developers.google.com/speed/pagespeed/service) seeks to address this and some other issues automatically.

Another website speed factor is server location. If your customers are half way across the world from your servers, any requests and transfers have to travel all that way, adding delay. By using servers located close to your audience, you can minimise this delay.

A neat service that helps in this area is Cloudflare. Cloudflare seeks to help optimise website speed in a number of ways, including through their optimizer and CDN (Content Delivery Network) which stores caches of your sites in each of its data centres around the world. When someone visits your site, the files are sent from the closest data centre, saving them from having to travel across the world. Cloudflare is free for basic accounts, and relatively easy to set up, so it's definitely worth a look.

Increasing website speed is too important to ignore but for most business owners addressing these sort of issues themselves is an ineffective and unprofitable use of time. If your tech team are able to implement the suggestions here for a cost, it's usually worth it.

How to create promotional videos in 10 minutes

Promotional videos can be useful in lots of ways:
- For use on your website to increase time on page. If you have a prominently-positioned video which explains what you do and the benefits of doing business with you, this can not only give visitors a quick intro to your business but will also keep them on the page longer, increasing the chance that they'll have a browse around.
- To boost conversion. Videos can help increase your conversion rate, for example by describing

the reasons why visitors should sign up, claim an offer or get in touch with you. Because people are generally lazy, you'll find that some who are unwilling to read text will happily sit and watch a short video that breaks up the message and feeds it to them in a more digestible way.

- For visibility on video sites. YouTube is the world's second largest search engine and a lot of people will turn straight to YouTube when they want to learn something. If you offer a product or service that requires your consumers to be educated about how to make a suitable choice, you'd better be sure that you're the one providing the education! Once you understand the basics of SEO, getting good visibility on YouTube is not hard and can be very rewarding.
- For visibility in search. Not only can videos themselves rank in search results, but they can also boost the ranking of your website. Google likes to show sites with 'rich media' on, and if your video title and description are keyword rich, popular and linked to your site, that page will be seen to have a higher value.
- For good quality inbound links to your website. By creating promotional videos with optimised titles and descriptions containing links to your website, you're building links from a good quality source that can attract qualified traffic.

In the past, promotional videos relied on expensive filming and editing teams. They took time out of yours and your staff's day, and were slow to create. If you needed changes made down the line, refilming was required and the whole process was slow and painful.

Fast forward to 2014, and thanks to websites like Animoto.com, promo videos are quick, easy and cheap (even free) to produce. Animoto allows you to create text and picture videos set to music. You can write text to form the basis for slides, add in some pictures and let the software do the rest, compiling the slides and pictures into a finished, professional looking video.

Once the video is created you can download a copy to upload to the various video sites. When we're creating and syndicating promotional videos for clients, we use YouTube.com, dailymotion.com, metacafe.com and vimeo.com.

Avoid using Generic stock images

There are two reasons we don't recommend the use of generic stock images. The first reason is a perception one. The business that uses stock images to sell itself is screaming "generic", and unfortunately that's not an appealing marketing message. The obvious exception is stock images that don't *look* like stock images. But if you're a dentist's surgery using that same brown haired girl with the perfect smile that's used on thousands of other websites selling everything from weight loss pills to male enhancements, unfortunately the association your customers will make is that you are of the same ilk.

Many small and medium sized businesses assume that their website needs to make them look like a large company, so tend to favour the generic look in their marketing. While it's important to appear well-established and stable, this can be achieved with good quality professional photos without having to remove the personality that sets their business apart in the first place. Professional, good. Generic, bad.

Ask any accountant if they have many clients that they've never met or spoken to, and they'll usually react with horror. For many accounting customers, it's important to feel that they know the accountant well and can trust them. That personal relationship is really important in this type of market, and face to face meetings are part of everyday life as a result.

And yet visiting these accountant's websites, you'd think they were operated by robots. It can be a challenge finding any pictures of the man or woman in charge, and the text and pictures are so generic that *of course* you'll have to meet them face to face, because you still have no idea who the person behind the site really is!

If you believe that personality is important in your business, then ask yourself how much personality comes across on your website, and if that is consistent. Replacing any generic stock images is a very good start…

Structure your About Us page to focus on benefits

If potential customers want to find out more information about your business, one of the pages that they might visit is your About Us page. But they're not really interested in finding out about *you* as much as they're interested in finding out how you can *help them*. A common mistake is to treat the About Us page as an information page, rather than a sales asset. But every inch of your website should be considered a sales asset and your About page is no exception.

So rather than talking only about your company's history, team and structure, remain laser focussed on benefits. If your company is well established, make it clear why this is important and the years of experience you have to draw from. If your company is new, this can also be positioned as a benefit. Perhaps you noticed a gap in the market not being filled by the existing big players, who were too slow to react or who didn't offer a compelling enough service so you felt forced to set up in business yourself.

When you talk about your team, it's an opportunity not only to sell them to your visitors but also give them credit for the value they bring to your organisation. Make them proud to share the page they're featured on. Pride in team members comes across well to customers and demonstrates your confidence in the business.

SEO

SEO, or Search Engine Optimisation is one of the cornerstones of a successful online marketing strategy. High ranking for relevant searches on Google, Bing and other search engines is many business's number one online marketing goal, and with good reason. High volumes of qualified traffic from prominent search positioning can transform a business, and we've been a part of some incredible success stories. Search Engine Optimisation is about organising the information about your business in your website in a way that gives Google and the other search engines what they want.

In the last couple of years the world of SEO has seen huge changes as Google modernises its algorithms and aims to improve the results it gives searchers. Consequently, the bar has raised for website owners and it's now much more difficult to artificially manipulate rankings than it was pre-2012. SEO has moved on from the days of trying to 'trick' Google on to what we all should have been focussing on in the first place: making our websites as useful as possible for users, and promoting them in a natural way around the internet.

In this section we'll be sharing our top SEO tips to boost your website's visibility and boost your organic ranking based on our experience promoting clients' sites in every possible market.

Create Separate Pages targeting each different keyword/service

If your business offers a range of products or services, giving each one their own separate page benefits you in three ways:

1. Separate pages allow you to organise your thoughts and make sure you're properly listing the features, benefits and typical uses of each product or service in adequate detail.
2. Visitors to your website can see the information in an organised and easy-to-read format.
3. Search engine optimisation on each of the pages can be more focussed towards keywords suitable for each product or service. Sites with more information and a higher number of pages also tend to rank higher than those who try to cram all the information onto fewer (but longer) pages.

If your products or services justify a lot of information, don't be afraid to provide it on your website. When it comes to SEO, the more information you can provide, the better. The key is to balance having a lot of information with making sure your pages don't become so long that readers are intimidated, and click away. Consider using expandable accordions to give readers access to more information without having it overwhelm them on the initial page load. Another alternative is to break the information into separate pages, for example splitting features, typical uses and specifications onto their own pages. This can help your readers quickly find the information they need, and also avoids forcing them to scroll through the information that they're *not* interested in.

Understand Your Customer's Language

This tip is just as relevant to SEO as general marketing, and it sounds too obvious to warrant much attention. Yet you'd be amazed how many businesses we consult with who don't know which which words and phrases their customers use to find their products or services. One of the most common mistakes is targeting only technical phrases, even if they are typically only used internally within the industry.

Searches based around the specific *benefits* or *features* that your product offers ("Passat exhaust repair") might perform better for you than searches describing what you are ("Volkswagen approved garage"). This is especially true for one-off purchases made by customers who might not understand your business or industry at all.

If you're not sure what customers would search to find you, here are 3 ways to start building a list of ideas:
1. Take a look at what your *competitors* think customers search for. Find your most prominent competitors on Google (these are usually the most switched on competitors, so if you're going to use someone as a reference it might as well

119

be these guys). Right click an empty area of their website and click View Source… A page of code will open, and you are looking for a section that starts `<meta name="keywords" content="`… The stuff that goes between the quote marks in the content=" section is the keywords that they are targeting. These aren't necessarily the *right* words to target, but you might get some good ideas.

2. Talk to your existing customers and ask them what they would search for to find you? Be careful not to subconsciously plant ideas in their heads ("what would you search for if you were searching for *nutrition courses in Kansas City*?"). Also listen out for the language prospective customers use in their initial enquiries, as the phrases they use are yet to be converted to technical speak during the buying process.

3. Head over to the Google Adwords Keyword Planner (https://adwords.google.com/ko/KeywordPlanner/Home) enter your website address, list the services you offer and define the areas you want to target. You'll then get a list of suggested keywords which can give you a good place to start.

Once you're comfortable that you understand the words and phrases that your audience is using to find you, make sure that you use this language throughout your website and in any adverts you are running. It sounds so obvious but talking the same language as your audience *really* helps to build affinity. Our book How to Get to the Top of Google is the bestselling SEO book in the UK, despite not having 'SEO' in the title. Why? Because our target audience is not computer geeks who think about SEO. SEO might be the word *we* use, but all our audience wants is to *get to the top of Google*.

Analyse Your Competitors' SEO - Phase 1: The Basics

The great thing about SEO is that everything is public. There are no secrets that a few tools and some know-how can't reveal, so let's look at how you can take a peek under the cover and spy on your competitors' SEO.

Whether you have one particular website that you'd really like to knock off top spot, or you're in a fiercely competitive market being outgunned and outspent, there are only two elements distinguishing your rankings from those of your competitors:

Onsite Optimisation

Onsite optimisation is the name we give to everything on your website itself. From the text, page titles, navigation and domain to the code behind the scenes, onsite optimisation is all about giving Google exactly what it wants on your website itself.

Offsite Promotion

Offsite promotion covers everything on the rest of the Internet that shows search engines how popular and authoritative your website and business are. From the number of quality inbound links to your social media profiles, good offsite promotion is crucial for a high ranking highly competitive website.

The first step in analysing your competitors' SEO is taking a good look at how they are ranking for a range of phrases relevant to your market. The best way to analyse this is to spend a good 10-15 minutes doing various searches and making some observations:

- Are any of your competitors showing up repeatedly for a number of different searches?
- Are any of the searches you're doing bringing up maps results? If so, are the same businesses ranking well in these local listings as they are for the regular searches?
- What are the names and URLs of the *pages* which are ranking? Is it always the homepage that is ranking or are there other content pages?
- What are the Titles of the pages? Do they contain the search terms you entered, and if so, where? Are the search terms at the start of the page titles, for example?
- Is Google automatically broadening your search to include related terms? For example if you search "headlamp bulbs" you'll see Google include results using the phrase "headlight bulbs".
- Are there any additional features in the search results? Do some of the websites show up with

little pictures of the owners? (See 'Integrating Google+ Authorship Markup) Do some results have Google+ Local listing information like address and phone number?

- Do the websites that show up contain any of the search terms in the domain name itself? E.g. www.searchtermhere.com

Analyse Your Competitors' SEO - Phase 2: Their Websites

The next phases of your competitor analysis is to start clicking on some of these search results and having a look at the websites themselves. To begin with we'll be noticing our first impressions:

- Does this website look good quality, trustworthy and reliable?
- How modern is the design? What impression does it make about the business? (e.g. fun, established, expensive, transparent, friendly, professional)
- Is it immediately clear what the business does, and who their target audience is?
- On the page that opens, can you see the phrase that you searched for?
- Is there a headline, and how effective is it at drawing you in?
- What do the pictures say?
- Does the page you landed on contain a lot of information relevant to someone performing the search you just did?

Generally, a website that contains a lot of information relevant to the target audience will tend to outrank one which skimps on the amount of text. You'll tend to find that the sites which are doing well in search results generally give quite a good experience to someone doing the sort of search you just performed, and the areas in which they excel give you really useful guidelines about how to improve your own ranking. The quality of websites themselves have a greater effect on ranking than ever before, and sites which cause visitors to 'bounce' away (immediately click back after visiting) tend to suffer poorer ranking than those who retain visitors and engage them more.

Analyse Your Competitors' SEO - Phase 3: Dig a Little Deeper

The next step is to take a closer look at your most prominent competitors' onsite SEO and start to look behind the scenes:

- Is the site's navigation clearly laid out, and can you see exactly where to find the information you need?
- Are there plenty of pages containing useful information in and around the topics that you've searched for? Do these pages use the phrase you searched for as well as related and alternative phrases?
- How often is your search phrase used on the landing page itself? Is it in the title?

- Are the business's contact details clearly visible on the site, or do you have to dig around to find them?

Next we're going to take a look at the hidden onsite elements. In a blank area of the page you landed on, right click and choose View Page Source.

- Do a search using ctrl+f (cmd+f on a mac) and type "Title". You should see the page's title highlighted. Notice if this page title contains the words or phrase you originally searched for, and where this is positioned in the title. You'll often see the target phrase right at the start of the title, and that's why this is one of the most valuable pieces of SEO real estate. For poorly optimised websites the Title will often just be the business name, which is a waste of such potentially valuable SEO space. Yes, the site will rank for the business name, but in all likelihood it would have anyway, so this space might as well be used to boost the site's ranking potential for their main target search.

- Next do a search for "description". You are looking for the section of code that starts `<meta="description" content="`... This is what's known as the Meta description and is a suggestion to search engines of what they might want to include in the website description in the search results. There's no guarantee that your Meta description will be shown, but it's good practice to treat it as an advert for your website

just in case. Notice if your competitors are using Meta descriptions on their sites and, if they are, how well written they are. Do they use real language or are they just a list of keywords? Is they long or short? Most search engines cut off Meta descriptions at 160 characters, so entire descriptions won't be shown if they're longer.

- Finally we're going to do a search for Meta keywords. This is a slightly redundant field that early search engines used to understand what a website was about and the practice has stuck. While Google has come out and openly said they don't use Meta keywords at all, there is some indication that Bing *does* still use them. Either way, by spying on your competitors' use of Meta keywords you can get an insight into the words and phrases that they've identified are most relevant. Do a search for "keywords" and look for a section starting `<meta="keywords" content="`...

- If you don't find either the Meta description or keywords sections, it's an indication that the site hasn't been fully optimised. This is great news.

- Finally, while we're still looking at the code of the homepage, search for your main target phrase to see how many times this is used in the content and code of the site. Perform the same search on the website itself (rather than the underlying code) to see how many times this phrase is used in the content. A well optimised site will include mentions of the main keyphrase as well as

variations, alternatives and any modifiers that
searchers might use (*compare*, *buy*, *reviews* etc)

If you carry out this research process for each of your
competitors' sites, you'll begin to build up a picture of
how well optimised the sites in your industry are. Most
business owners could do a lot worse than spend some
time digging around through search results and their
competitor's websites as this will be the battlefield that
future competition will take place on.

Analyse Your Competitors' SEO - Step 4: Back link analysis

The final step of your competitor analysis is to see how
much offsite SEO your competitors have engaged in.
There are various sites you can use to do this, but we're
going to be using two of our favourites. The first is Open
site Explorer (http://www.opensiteexplorer.org/). Open
site explorer allows you to get some limited information
about your competitors free of charge, with additional
info available if you want to pony up for Moz
membership. For the level of competitor analysis we'll
be covering here, the free version is adequate.

Head over to Open Site Explorer and stick your main
competitor's website address into the form and hit
search. Up will pop some statistics which can give us an
indication of the quality and volume of the inbound links:

- Domain authority is an indicator of the overall
  popularity of the site as a whole. The idea is to

mimic Google's Pagerank indicator, which is one of the ranking factors Google uses and is based on the number and quality of websites linking to your site. the higher the Pagerank or Domain authority, the higher the site will tend to rank.

- Page authority is the same measure, but on a page level so you can use it to see which of the pages on your site are the most linked to.
- The next interesting piece of information is under the Anchor Text tab. Anchor text is the text used in each link, for example a link that appears click here has the anchor text "click here". Typically, if a site has been participating in a lot of SEO, their anchor text profile will be quite unnatural and with some experience, you'll start to spot this a mile off. Usually sites naturally attract links that use either the business name or website URL as the anchor text. Links using keyword rich anchor text are links to your site that use the keywords you want to rank for, for example buy viagra online. These sort of links are actually very uncommon in the 'wild', so if you notice any of your competitors with a lot of exact match anchor text inbound links, you can be pretty sure that they've done at least *some* SEO.
- Next, under the Linking Domains tab you'll be able to see the sort of sites that are linking to each of your competitors, along with their authority scores. This can give you some good insights into any SEO they have done, and you can go back to the sites linking to them and have

a look at the context of the link. Did they write an article with a link appearing in the bio? Perhaps they commented on a blog? Is someone talking about them? The point here is to notice everything that your competitors are doing so that you can steal the best bits and implement them for yourself. If there are industry directories linking to their sites, you want to make sure that your business is listed in those categories too. If your competitors are writing articles for an industry magazine or blog, contact the owner to see if you can do the same. If they're active on social media, are they using any strategies that you can copy?

Use effective Meta descriptions

As mentioned above, Meta descriptions are short pieces of text that search engines sometimes use as the text description in search results. Every content page of your site should have its own unique Meta description and it's very important that your Meta descriptions are well optimised to include your target keywords and a good dose of juicy temptation for searchers to click on your link.

There are two goals for your Meta descriptions:
1. Demonstrate the relevance of your webpage to the searcher's query, and
2. Entice them to click on your site ahead of your competitors on the same page.

With that in mind, here are the Exposure Ninja tips for killer Meta description writing:

- Use your keywords in a natural way. There is no need to stuff the Meta description with too many instances of your keywords as it'll just make it read spammy and reduce click throughs.
- Keep benefits-focussed. Why should people visit your website or buy from you? What are the benefits of your product or service compared to the competitors you'll be up against on that search results page?
- Using testimonials in your Meta descriptions can work well. They're a really useful tool for saying what you'd be too shy to say about yourself, and if you have some that include your keywords you can use snippets rather than writing your own.
- Consider the context of your visitors' searches. If most of your target audience is searching for information, let them know that they can get plenty of information on your site by telling them so in your Meta description. If your audience is ready to buy, let them know if they can get free delivery, free gifts with an order, competitive pricing etc

How you edit your Meta descriptions depends how your website is build. If you're using a CMS (Content Management System), usually there will be a place to enter a description for each page in the admin area. In Wordpress, you can use a plugin such as All In One

SEO Pack to enable this functionality. If you're unsure how to implement Meta descriptions on your website, best to ask your website geek. If they are unresponsive or you don't like talking to them, drop us a line through http://exposureninja.com and we'll be happy to help.

Use Effective and optimised page titles

As we've already said, the titles of your pages are one of the most important things to optimise on your website. They're also one of the areas that are typically left behind by the vast majority of business owners, who use their business name as every page title thus wasting prime opportunities to boost ranking for really useful keywords.

The most important part of your page titles is the first few words in your homepage title. This is the area where you should be using your top keyword because this is a huge sign to Google that your website is super relevant for this phrase. Yes, you can use your business name in your homepage title, but use your keywords first.

A good guideline format is this:

Cupcake Shop Bristol | Tim's cakes in Clifton

This title does three things:
1. It uses our the main target keyphrase of Tim's imaginary cake shop, 'Cupcake shop bristol'
2. It includes the business name Tim's cakes
3. It includes a further geographic marker, Clifton.

Just like Meta descriptions, your page titles should be different for every page of your site. Use the primary target keywords for each page in the title to give that page the best chance of ranking.

Optimise your images and pictures for search

Ever wondered how Google knows which pictures to show when you type "cute guinea pigs" into Google images?

There are a number of things you can do to tell Google about what your images are showing, and doing this not only increases the chances of your pictures showing up in image search results (which can be a good source of traffic), but also boosts the optimisation of your site in general. Here's how to optimise your images for search:

- Use image alt tags. These are Meta data (i.e. they are visible only in the code, not to visitors) that are used to tell browsers what to show if a picture can't be displayed. Think that search engines use this information too? You betcha. So it's best to use your keywords in your alt tags whenever possible.
- Image titles. These are used to create a tooltip so when visitors hover their mouse over the picture, some text is displayed. Again, this text should be optimised for your target keywords.

- Image file name. Because this filename is usually used in the URL of the image itself, it's really important that the filename itself contains your keywords. www.website.com/images/fast+car.jpg is much easier for search engines to understand than www.website.com/images/3erjjjaii4214erljs_small.jpg
- Use captions where necessary. Images grab the eye and captions are the next place the eye is drawn to, so take advantage of this by making them strong, laden with benefits and, of course, use keywords so they're search optimised.

Increase the number of pages on your website

One of the biggest, juiciest pieces of low hanging fruit for most websites is simply the amount of content on the site.

It might not surprise you that 'big' websites (with lots of pages and lots of content) tend to outrank smaller sites. There are typically three reasons for this:
- More content on the site implies authority and increases the chance that your audience will find the information they are looking for to help them make a buying decision.
- More laser targeted pages increases the chance that they'll show up in search results, thus increasing your traffic.

- More pages generally means higher Pagerank. Pagerank is created with every new page and the more pages your site has, the more Pagerank will pass to your homepage. While this doesn't guarantee that your site will automatically rank higher, it does make it more likely.

Use Guest Blogging to Kill 3 Birds with One Stone

Guest blogging is the foundation of good quality link building in 2014. For those who aren't familiar, guest blogging is where you write for popular authority websites in your market. You can offer 'an insider's view' on a particular subject, write opinion pieces or talk about the latest news. So what are these three birds being taken out by the monster guest blogging stone?

1. Boost your credibility and authority. Your target audience are seeing you, a vendor, being positioned as a thought leader and authority industry figure. The reason they're visiting this website in the first place is to learn, and by being present in a place like this you immediately differentiate yourself and put your business head and shoulders above the competition.

2. Get some high quality, relevant, authority backlinks. This is the sweet sweet nectar of SEO. A link from a website relevant to your market, with plenty of good quality original content and lots of links from other sites in your industry.

134

Google wants to reward authority and by securing a link from sites like these, you're demonstrating that you have that authority.

3. Lastly, you're likely to pick up some qualified traffic from your guest blog posts. Obviously how much traffic you get depends on how tantalising the offer or pitch at the end of your article is, how much traffic your host site gets and how prominent your blog post is.

For tips on securing guest blogging opportunities, see "Finding PR Opportunities Online" in the Online Marketing section.

Use Google+ Authorship Markup To Boost Ranking and Stand Out in Search Results

While this tip is focussed on Google+ (a social network), we're including it in the SEO section because it's such a useful tool for attracting more clicks from search result pages.

Google+ is Google's Facebook competitor, and while Facebook is still undeniably king of the social networks, Google+ deserves Prince status for it's SEO benefits. We're going to be focussing on integration of something that Google+ calls 'Authorship markup'.

Authorship markup is part of Google's attempt to bring a more accurate measure of authority to internet content. The thinking is that if every website (and even individual pages) are linked to someone's social media profile, by measuring the authority of the profile Google can judge the likely authority of the page. In practice, we're still in the very early days of this type of associated authority but the signs are strong that it will continue to grow and there are already some benefits to being an early adopter.

The two main benefits of Google+ Authorship markup are:
1. Increased ranking in searches performed by people connected to you.
2. Your picture and name can show up in the search results next to your website. This can significantly increase click through rates (CTR)

Let's look at each in turn:

Boost ranking for Google+ connections

Google understands that a recommendation from someone familiar holds more weight than recommendations from people we don't know. If your next door neighbour recommends a local restaurant to you, their familiarity will tend to give their endorsement more weight than a recommendation from someone you've never seen before two streets down. There's no rational explanation for this, but that's how it works.

Authorship markup is a way for Google to show you websites authored and +1'd by people who are connected to you on Google+. For those people, your site will rank significantly higher - usually first page for relevant phrases. Obviously you're not going to be connected to every single searcher, so the ranking benefits are limited BUT successful SEO is about lots of small effects compounded, and this is too important to ignore.

Visibility for your Name and Picture

An example of a successfully linked website and Google+ profile is shown below:

Face Painter Southampton. Moxie's Magical Faces Children's and ...
facepaintersouthampton.co.uk/ ▼
by Zoe Moxie
Face Painter in **Southampton** Moxie's Magical Faces. Children's **face painting**, adult **face painting**, parties and games from experienced entertainer Zoe Moxie.

This listing stands out a mile on the search results page, and not just because it's ranked top. Studies show a 30-150% increase in Click Through Rate when using this type of markup, so the potential benefits are significant.

The increase in CTR will obviously depend on a number of variables including:
- How attractive/relevant your picture is. In Zoe's example above, you can see that the search is for a face painter so having her face painted in the authorship picture is highly relevant.
- How familiar your audience is with you. If you're a well-respected authority in your field, that

familiarity will significantly increase your CTR amongst those who are familiar with your work
- How personality-driven your business is. If your business is heavily dependent on trust and personal relationships (think accountants, solicitors, personal trainers) then having your face showing in the SERPs is a great way to start building familiarity before searchers even reach your site.

Implementing Authorship Markup

The first step is to sign up for a personal Google+ account. Head to Google.com/+ and go through the sign up process. When it comes to choosing a photo it's important to use a clearly recognisable well lit headshot so people can see your face. Some of the tradesmen clients we work with send us headshot photos to use that look like mug shots or Crimewatch CCTV stills, in which case we have to explain nicely that the point of the picture is to *entice* clicks.

Once your profile is complete, follow the instructions on https://plus.google.com/authorship to finalise the markup.

Integrating a Google+ Business Page with your Website

Having a Google+ Business page linked to your site gives Google the option to use business information in the search results, as seen in the local example below:

You'll notice that there's an address marker below the website listing, then the larger map listing on the right hand side populated with information from the business's Google+ Local page.

For non-local businesses, similar benefits are available:

In this example you'll see that information is being taken from Oracle's Google+ Business page (Recent posts, number of followers) as well as from elsewhere on the Internet.

Just as with Google+ Authorship markup, the first step is to set up a Google+ Business page in the correct category. Head to https://plus.google.com/pages/create and choose the appropriate category to get started.

Once your page is completed fully, add the following to each page on your website (we tend to do it in the footer so it's inobtrusive) <a href="https://plus.google.com/yourpageID" rel="publisher">Find us on Google+</a>
Substitute the link in quotes for your Google+ Business profile, then head into your profile and add your website address. You'll see a button to 'Link Website' and clicking this will trigger Google to check for the reciprocal link back from your website. Alternatively you can link the site through your analytics account, or by using an email address that matches your website's domain. For more information see https://support.google.com/webmasters/answer/170884 4?hl=en

Use Directory Listings to improve your ranking and visibility

Local and market-specific directories are a great source of backlinks as well as potential customers. But the emphasis must be on targeting *quality* directories only.

Because of the SEO benefits of obtaining back links from directories, thousands of low quality 'junk' directories were established for people who just wanted backlinks and didn't care about the relevance. Google took a look at these junk directories, decided that the Internet would be a better place without them, and adjusted its ranking algorithms to ignore or penalise links from them.

But this doesn't damage the effectiveness of genuinely *good quality* directories that actually serve a purpose for consumers. Such directories include Yell, Brownbook, Yelp and Fyple, as well as the many region-specific directories you will find listing businesses in your local area. While this type of directory is mainly targeted at local businesses, there are usually directories specific to each market which provide a similar relevance to users looking for a company in your category.

How to find good quality directories

The best way to find good quality directories is, unsurprisingly, Google. With three Google searches, you can find all the most suitable local directories:

1. "<Your area> directory". Local directories are great for boosting your visibility in the local area and can sometimes have a strong local base of users.

2. "<Your Industry> directory". This search will bring up the best quality directories specific to your market.
3. "Business directory". General business directories can provide quite authoritative links, as can local chamber of commerce and business networks.

If Google ranks a directory fairly highly in its search results, it's reasonably safe to assume that it's considered good quality. But just to be on the safe side, you should still use your own judgement and ask the following questions:

- Is this directory designed for real people, or just web geeks looking for backlinks? The clue is often in the title - if the words "SEO" or "Link" are used in the title, it's a fairly safe bet that the directory exists purely for low quality SEO.
- If you were looking for a business and you found this directory, would you use it or would you click away? If the site is useful and good quality, great. If it looks spammy or low quality, best to avoid it.
- Is there a review process for new listings? The highest quality directories have a manual review process to prevent spammy listings. If a directory allows every listing, quality or not, then it'll inevitably be targeted by spammers and eventually ignored or punished by Google.
- Are there signs that the directory has some sort of business model, for example premium listings, extra services or a charitable association?

Directories without any visible signs of a business model should arouse suspicion. They could be selling contact details and are best avoided.

When creating directory listings, your goal should be to submit as much information as possible. Not only does this increase the quality of the listing page in Google's eyes, but it can also give your listing an advantage in the directory itself. Most directories want to show users the most complete listings because they're the ones likely to be correct and useful to visitors. So adding pictures, a good description and your contact details is a very good idea.

To boost the visibility of your local Google+ listing if you're a local business, make sure to include your business name address and phone number *exactly* as it appears on your website and Google+ Local page. This is what's known as a 'citation', and it's treated like a sort of local version of a backlink. As a result, businesses that have a lot of citations tend to outrank those that don't.

Obtain backlinks from suppliers using Testimonials

Most SEO training suggests that website owners contact clients and suppliers asking for links back to their websites. But most people can't face the awkwardness of asking for favours like this, and even for those that can, they usually find the supplier or customer requests a reciprocal link. This means that not only do you have to clutter your site with links, but reciprocal links hold less weight, and are of limited use.

We have a solution to get around this. For any of your contacts that have a testimonials page on their site, you can offer a testimonial that they can use and include a link back to your site. They win by getting another great testimonial and you win by getting the link.

Use Tradeshow appearances to boost your visibility online

Trade or consumer show appearances are a great source of leads and a good opportunity to network. But they also offer a great way to secure some juicy backlinks.

Tradeshow websites tend to have quite high authority because a lot of industry blogs and suppliers' sites link to them. When you're negotiating the fee for your pitch, it's worth requiring a guest blog or feature on their website. If you wait to make this demand just before arranging payment, the salesperson will often comply because they want the sale, and the website has relatively low importance in their mind. Just as with placing magazine articles you want to do as much of the work for them as possible, so write the guest post or feature for them and make sure to include your link as they won't think to add it.

Set up a Sitemap

A sitemap tells search engines about all the pages on your site. While modern search engines are generally pretty good at finding their way around websites and picking up each page, a sitemap is good SEO practice and can allow Google to crawl and index pages that are less easy to find, such as landing pages that aren't linked from your main navigation.

The process of setting up a sitemap is made infinitely easier if you are using a content management system (CMS) like Wordpress, as there are readymade plugins that will create your sitemap in the correct format and with just a few clicks, such as Google XML Sitemaps.

If you're not using a CMS, building a Sitemap is a bit more work and something that your web team will need to do. By all means drop us a line if you'd like some help with this.

Link your website to Google Webmaster Tools

Once you've built your sitemap and optimised your site's content, the next step is to link it through Webmaster Tools.

Go to Google.com/webmasters and follow the sign up process to create your webmaster account. Once you've done this you'll see an option to Add A Site. Enter your site's URL and follow the instructions verify ownership of your website.

Once you've verified ownership of your website you'll want to submit your sitemap. In your main webmaster dashboard you'll see a section called Sitemaps. By clicking on the heading you'll see a button that says Add/Test Sitemap. Drop in the URL of your sitemap and click Submit sitemap. After a couple of seconds you'll see an option to refresh the page and this should show you that your sitemap has been successfully submitted.

The next step is to submit your site to Google's index. You should see a menu on the left hand side of the page. Click Crawl to expand the menu and choose the Fetch as Google option. Once the page loads you'll see your site's URL with a red box that says Fetch. Click this box and you'll see a button titled Submit to index appear. Click this and you'll get the option to submit your site to Google's index. Choose the *URL and all linked pages* option to submit your entire site (rather than just the homepage) to the index. Simple!

Understand the difference between good and bad links

Google uses the links pointing at each website to assess its authority. If lots of websites link to your website, it appears to be more important and have higher authority. Higher authority websites tend to receive higher ranking, so until relatively recently the name of the game was simply to get as many links as possible pointing at your site.

This led to some extremely aggressive and quite inventive ways of automating the creation of billions of links across the internet through blog comments, low quality directories, junk articles and hacked websites.

Google reacted by changing its algorithm to ignore or even punish those who were responsible for 'spamming' these links. The writing had been on the wall for a while but with Google's Penguin update, millions of websites lost the ranking they had come to rely on as a source of business literally overnight.

Since the quality of links started having a significant effect on ranking, it has been really important to understand the difference between good and bad links. Good links can help your ranking and bring you traffic, while bad links can potentially harm your ranking.

Simply, a good link is one that appears natural: you could imagine the link existing without any intervention from someone trying to boost ranking. Such links could be contained in forum posts, articles on news or magazine websites, good quality directories, blog posts and, yes, even in blog comments. Natural links don't usually exist on their own, there's usually some writing around them and the writing usually relates to the subject of the website being linked. The websites that natural links appear on tend to be good quality and visited by real humans.

By contrast, spammy links are often posted on low quality sites, or good quality sites that contain a lot of other spammy links. They tend to use anchor text which matches exactly the words or phrase that the website owner wants to rank for. The text around the link is usually gibberish or is exactly the same as the text surrounding hundreds of *other* links to the exact same website. This leaves a very definite *footprint* which Google can use to safely assume that automated link building software, rather than a human being, is responsible for the link.

Here is a concise summary of the main distinguishing features of what we consider to be good and bad links:
Good links:
- Exist on websites relevant to the topic of the linked site.
- Use natural anchor text, typically the name of the business or name of the website. rather than the keyword the website wants to rank for.
- Are surrounded by natural, unique and related text.
- Appear on a mixture of high authority and low authority sites - a natural spread.

Bad links:
- Exist on websites spammed to oblivion by other spammy comments.

- Use anchor text that matches exactly the words or phrase the the linked site wants to rank for.
- Are surrounded by gibberish or text that is duplicated across other sites on the net.
- Tend to appear mostly in a number of 'giveaway' forms: blog comments, articles or forum posts (because these are simple to create automatically using software).
- Usually have no relevance to the subject of the host site.
- Appear on sites that serve no useful purpose to humans, other than those trying to build links.

Stay clear of Google Penalties

Ranking penalties are disturbing to see. Trying to overturn ranking penalties is part of our daily life. As a rule they're easier to avoid than they are to fix, so the best plan is to steer clear of them in the first place.

Here are our top tips for avoiding the wrath of Google and staying clear of ranking penalties:
- SEO itself is not bad, and Google itself approves of and supports legitimate SEO. But choose your SEO company as carefully as you choose where to eat on a night out: you probably wouldn't want to put the world's cheapest kebab anywhere near your mouth, and the best you can hope for from cheap SEO companies is that they take your money and *do nothing*. God forbid they use the link building tools they bought in 2008 or you can cancel your hosting, pack up and go home.

- If you decide to try your SEO on your own, that's OK. But don't start looking for shortcuts. Any tools that promise to help you build links, or services to buy backlinks are the exact same tools and services that Google's smartest geeks are working night and day to punish and eliminate. Don't let their appearance and friendly logo fool you - you stand more chance in a duel with a hungry polar bear.
- When you're analysing sites to build links on, whether they're directories, magazine or news sites or blogs that you'd like to write for, ask yourself whether this is a good quality site that you would really want to use. If it looks a bit junk, don't risk it.
- Avoid any promotion or SEO company that doesn't tell you explicitly up front what sort of links they're going to be building. Our penalty recovery clients send us reports from the SEO companies that got them penalised and there's *no* detail. It's as if the company is doing absolutely *nothing* each month (ironically that would have been more beneficial in the long term). SEO is important so be diligent about finding out exactly what their plan is to promote your site.

If you suspect that you've been hit by a penalty, recovery is beyond the scope of this book. However, we do offer a completely free of charge assessment with recommendations over at http://exposureninja.com, and

150

we have some blog posts on the site which deal with this topic in more detail.

Deserve to rank highly

While much of SEO in the past was focussed on manipulation of search rankings to rank sites higher than they deserve, business owners spend very little time on actually improving what their website offers in order to give users more of what they want.

If you're a small E-commerce store competing with Amazon and other well-established online retailers, you need to ask the very honest question of whether or not you actually *deserve* to outrank them. Google wants to show users the most useful and relevant search results, and the truth is that for many smaller sites, the experience they offer users is inferior to the experience of their competitors.

Let's compare a product page on Amazon to a product page on a typical small E-commerce store product page:

Small E-commerce store product page:
- Product name, using the exact name used elsewhere on the Internet for the same product
- Product description, typically copy and pasted from the manufacturer/distributor's description (thus duplicate content and nothing new)
- Product images

- Price (typically the same as on the other sites selling the product

Amazon product page:
- Product name
- Clickable manufacturer link
- Summary of main product features
- Product description (often much more detailed and including pictures)
- Detailed trustworthy customer reviews
- Links to second hand buying options
- Pricing for new and second-hand versions
- A link to customer pictures
- Links to related products viewed and purchased by others who viewed this product (relevant and useful)
- Links to the store that the product is in, as well as links to related special offers from that store
- Delivery and availability information
- Product rank according to category and a link to the category bestseller list
- Links to customer discussions about the product
- Links to find similar items by category
- Links to your recent viewing history
- Links to products related to those in your viewing history
- Links to returns and exchange information

When comparing these two pages then, it's relatively easy to see how Google's algorithms might judge the

Amazon page more relevant and useful to searchers, and decide to rank it higher.

This isn't to say that it's impossible to outrank Amazon or larger sites for competitive searches, and we've even helped clients successfully outrank brands for their own phrases, so it can be done. But the first step is to offer something additional or more valuable than the page you are competing with. Whether this is carefully curated content, advice or professional expertise, you need to have the ammunition to fight against a player like Amazon, and a copycat site just won't cut it.

The truth is that many site owners simply aren't willing to *truly* compete. They'd rather spend a lot of money chasing ineffective shortcuts to avoid using an ounce of work or originality. This is good news for you because it's likely that at least some of your competitors have this mindset, but be careful not to fall into the trap of it yourself. You don't have to reinvent the wheel, but you *should* seek to offer website visitors something unique or that is an improvement on what they get from your competitors.

Avoid Duplicate Content

Copying and pasting can seem like a really quick and easy shortcut to writing lots of text for your website, particularly if you have lots of pages (for example a large E-commerce store).

The trouble is that Google is like the ever-knowing school teacher: they *always* know when you've been copying someone's homework. And those who copy homework (or product descriptions) are generally lazy and naughty. Just like the teacher gives no marks for copied homework, duplicate content gets no brownie points from Google.

The same goes for content copied from other pages on your site. A classic example is a local business that has pages targeting a number of different local areas. To save time, they often copy the text across each page, changing just the name of the area. They'd make the reasonable point that the services they offer in each area are exactly the same so it's perfectly reasonable to copy pages across. Perfectly reasonable, maybe, but not optimal from an SEO point of view.

It's not just duplicate content on your website that you have to be careful about though. Back in the spammy SEO days of article marketing, it was common practice to create one article and upload it across dozens of different article sites. This would create lots of backlinks for the work of creating only one article. Ideal!

But then Google started flagging duplicate content like this, so the spammers adapted and began using 'spinners' that would slightly alter the text of the articles to try and escape detection by Google's algorithms. Seen those jumbled nonsense blog comments your site gets hammered with? These are often the result of comments 'spun' so far that they no longer make sense. All of this means that Google has had a lot of practice identifying duplicate content, and it's generally beyond the skills of us mere mortals to fool it.

Our advice is to manually rewrite any content that you need to 'copy' to another location. That means different headings and actually rewriting the text from scratch.

Finding duplicate content

The tool we use to find content that has been duplicated across the web is www.copyscape.com. Using Copyscape, you can enter a URL and have the service search the web for pages that match the text on the site. If you upgrade to a pro account (which is very inexpensive) you can paste in text and have Copyscape scan the text for this text, as well as have it search multiple URLs at once, and automatically scan for new duplicated content at a set interval.

Accidental duplicate content

Not all duplicated content is intentional, and there is one case in particular where accidental duplication of an entire website can happen.

Google treats http://domain.com and www.domain.com as two separate websites, and the problems start when neither one is chosen as the primary website location, and both exist in parallel. Although you and I know that this is the same website, Google sees it as two website with exactly the same content. The correct setup is to choose one or the other to be the website destination (it doesn't matter which, but generally you want to choose the one that has the most links pointing to it), and set up the other to automatically forward traffic to it.

How you do this will depend on your domain settings. For more information or help doing this, just drop us a line and we'll be more than happy to help out.

Use 'Pretty' URLS

Next time you are surfing the web, notice the page URLs that different sites use. If we take an example from Amazon: http://www.amazon.co.uk/How-Get-Top-Google-including-ebook/dp/B0076XVNM8 you can probably take a fairly decent stab at what that page contains, even without clicking the link.

Another example, this time from Exposure Ninja: http://exposureninja.com//our-marketing-services/seo/seo-consultation/
No prizes at all for guessing what that page is about just from reading the link.

By contrast, let's shame Google themselves by taking a look at the absolutely shocking format of the links in their Google+ social network: https://plus.google.com/101692259663878568802/posts

That, friends, is revolting. The only thing that we can judge from that is that it's something to do with Google+ and there are probably some posts. To be completely fair to Google, they've recently unveiled custom Google+ URLs, allowing people to choose the bit to replace those horribly unfriendly numbers. But still, it's been long enough.

'Pretty' URLs are useful for 3 main reasons:

1. They show Internet users what a page is about without them having to click the link, whether they see the URL in search results, in a comment, email or anywhere else.

2. They're a great place to put your keywords to show Google what your page is about. When they show up in the search results, the words that match your query will be highlighted in bold as well, for some extra 'standing out' points.

3. They're dead easy to use anytime you want someone to copy them into your browser. For example: Visit http://exposureninja.com/101 to claim your FREE 7 Point Online Marketing Review from our world-class experts. If that link said http://exposureninja.com/130992n_234o?=23498 239fgdkhDSA how many would be rushing to their computer's to claim the audit? We haven't tested it, but I'd be willing to bet the answer would be 'fewer'.

If you're using Wordpress, pretty URLs are as simple as going to Settings => Permalinks and choosing Post name. If you're not using Wordpress, your process will be different. Give us a shout if you need any help with your permalinks and we'll be glad to advise free of charge.

Local SEO

For most local searches, Google now shows map listings with (usually) seven businesses listed. Obviously, placement in this list is highly coveted and the strategies that we use to rank businesses well in local results are the subject of this section.

Take Ownership of your Google+ Local Page

Many local businesses already have a Google+ Local (what used to be called Google Places) page, but often these have been automatically generated by Google and are not managed by the business itself.

There are a number of advantages to claiming your Google+ Local listing, including being able to link it to your website, add pictures and videos, update contact information and write a nice detailed description mentioning the products and services you offer.

If your unclaimed listing is already showing up in Google search results, click on the listing and you'll notice a

'Manage this Page' button towards the bottom. This will take you through the verification process, which usually involves requesting a postcard with PIN number or an automated phone call to your business phone line to make sure that you're the authorised business owner.

If your listing isn't showing up, or you're not sure if Google has an automatically-generated listing for your business, you can try creating a new listing. If Google finds duplicate details in their system, they'll ask if you'd like to manage the existing page rather than creating a new page. Go to https://www.google.com/local/business/ and click Add a listing to get started. You'll be asked to search for your business, and if you can't find it click the option to add your business from scratch.

When you're managing your Google+ Local page it's best to include as much information as possible because Google tends to favour fully completed listings. So make sure to add pictures, videos, opening times, contact information and anything else you can possibly cram into that page to give Google exactly what it wants.

Establish a Process for Obtaining Reviews from Customers

In Germany, Alpecin shampoo use the slogan "Doping fur die haare" (Doping for your hair). If caffeinated shampoo is doping for your hair, then you can consider collecting reviews as doping for your business. And it should be every local business's goal to become the Lance Armstrong of review collection.

Getting your customers to leave reviews on your Google+ page is a great way to boost your local visibility and attract more clicks to your site. But the main obstacle for most businesses is creating a *system* for review collection. Early on they might ask a select few customers for a review on their page, then every so often they'll do another spurt of requests, but there's not a fixed repeatable system in place, seriously limiting the number of reviews that they collect.

Such a system doesn't have to be hard work to build or implement and, with a little bit of creativity, it can even run automatically. Of course you're collecting customer information for your database, so as part of an autoresponder sequence (see Online Marketing section) one of your early automated emails can be a simple request to leave a review along with a link to your Google+ page, Tripadvisor page, Trustpilot or any other review site that you are targeting.

If you've dealt with a customer who is particularly happy with your service, or you've gone out of your way and want to make the most of the goodwill you've generated, ask *"if you think we've done a good job for you, would you be willing to leave a short review on our Google+ page (link)? It really helps us grow our business and show potential customers what sort of service we offer"*.

If you or your team follows up with customers or clients after the sale is made, ask for a review. If you sell or deliver physical product, drop a "Will you review us?" postcard in with each purchase.

However you ask for your reviews, focus on making it as easy as possible for your customers to do them. Google+ page URLs are long and difficult to type correctly, so you might consider making a /reviews page on your website which has links to the different review sites you want to direct customers to.

Create pages on your website to target each location

One of the main challenges for local businesses that target a number of different local areas is including enough quality and relevant content on their websites to target each individual area.

One of our local clients offers a wedding planning service to a number of different counties around London. The challenge in this type of case is to rank the business in an area outside of where it is located.

Because we're competing against actual local competitors situated in the towns and cities we are targeting, there are some things that we just can't do. an example is Google+ Local ranking. Unless a local business has an office (or virtual office) in each town, it's extremely unlikely that the Google+ page will show up on maps far outside its area. However, organic SEO and PPC are still useful.

To target organic SEO, what we'll typically do is set up pages on the site targeted at each local area. These pages will be optimised for the area and include plenty of locally-relevant content. For the wedding planning business above, what we did was set up a page for each of the target areas and write a guide to getting married in that area. We used links to different local wedding venues and suppliers, and wrote about the different styles of weddings popular in each area. The result is a set of highly optimised pages targeting a wide area, but with focussed locally relevant content.

So if you need to target lots of local areas, work out what sort of targeted content you can create which will be genuinely useful to each of the local audiences. Putting this content on distinct pages will give them more chance of ranking well in each area, and also builds more affinity with your audience.

Social Media

Social media marketing gives businesses an unprecedented opportunity to read, participate and even *shape* organic word of mouth conversations. Because it's relatively new on the scene, most social media marketing is little short of guesswork. But it doesn't have to be like this.

The key to an effective social media marketing campaign is setting out with a goal in mind, and being willing to invest during the early stages when your audience is still growing.

In this section we'll present our top social media tips to build and farm your audience.

Be present on social media, whether or not you'll use it to sell

Twitter is not just about self centered celebrity and Facebook is not just about pictures with amusing captions. Social media is a useful tool for every single business with an online presence for three main reasons:

1. It gives potential customers reassurance that there's a public face, should they have any problems. A social media feed on your website is a reassuring sign of life - it's like the beating heart in the online body. It shows visitors that you're online and responsive which is really

useful to build credibility and trust in an otherwise anonymous business.

2. Google uses social signals as a ranking factor. Businesses with active social media channels, lots of engagement and plenty of sharing tend to rank better. If the thought of 'lots of engagement' fills you with dread, fear not. You can get many of the positive SEO effects of social media by setting up profiles linked to your site, creating Google+ business and personal pages and encouraging visitors to share, Tweet and like your website and content.

3. It can be a powerful source of social proof. By responding to questions and talking to clients and potential clients openly on social media, you are sending a signal to other potential buyers that you're a 'safe' business to deal with. Online it's not always obvious who the most reliable companies are, so anything you can do to tilt the scales in your favour will help add to your appeal. Positive conversations with clearly happy customers is one of the most powerful ways to grab some social proof.

Therefore, we encourage every business to experiment with social media, even if they're not sure that their audience is heavy users. First mover advantage is significant, and if you're one of the first in your industry to really embrace social media, you can establish your profiles as the place people go to for up to date information.

Make benefits statements clear on all social profiles

Benefit statement are the short sentences or phrases that concisely state the benefit of your product or service. Clearly displaying a benefit statement or 5 on your website is a good start, but don't forget that your social media profiles are also very visible and should not be neglected. A good question to ask is:

Can visitors to our Facebook/Twitter/Google+ page see exactly what we offer, and who our target audience is, within 3 seconds?

You might be surprised just how many business social media pages neglect this basic information. It's not uncommon for us to be sent a Facebook page for a local business that lacks information about the area served, the target audience and even sometimes the core product or service! These social profiles are effectively landing pages for your business, so all the same rules should apply as for landing pages on your website. And above all, focus on the benefits!

Use controversy in your Social Media Marketing

Controversy is a useful tool in the savvy marketer's arsenal. Picking fights against enemies of your audience is a great way to align yourself with them and raise your profile. Done right, controversy doesn't even have to be controversial!

Almost every group of customers has a common enemy. Typically this will be one or more of the following:

The 'old guard' and tradition

Does your audience identify with a new way of working that the traditional providers stand against? For example we've often compared web marketing very favourably against old fashioned marketing channels such as Yellow Pages, that many of our clients have grown sceptical of.

The new guard or new competitors and solutions

Perhaps your customers appreciate the way things have always been done and are reluctant to change. Can you align your business with this mindset by exposing the flaws in a new technology or innovation?

Customer ignorance

For B2B companies, customer ignorance can be one of your clients' most frustrating business challenges, taking many forms. From plumbers frustrated that their unregistered and unqualified competitors are booked solid, to high end furniture stores frustrated by customers choosing IKEA, being seen to take on such perceived ignorance and educate people on behalf of your clients can give you massive credibility and rapport in your market.

Legislation and regulations

Does your audience resent legislation and regulatory interference? If so, by declaring your allegiance and stepping forward as the champion of the cause, you take a shortcut straight into their consciousness and favour. This epitomises the 'find a parade to stand in front of' mentality, and can be *very* effective.

The Government

Don't be afraid to get political, but only if you're *certain* that you are aligning yourself with your audience. Proclaiming your conservative beliefs to a liberal audience will break rapport just as fast as it would build rapport for an audience that matches your ideals. A lower risk strategy is to targeting particular policies that work against your market.

The Economy

If all else fails, blame the economy. While you can *use* this message to align yourself with customers hit hard by economic conditions, don't allow yourself to actually fall prey to the associated victim mindset.

Controversy Doesn't Have to be Controversial

If you're not the type with a stomach for a public argument but you still want to tap into the positioning power of a good dose of controversy, there is a solution. By careful opponent selection you can eliminate all chances of a response.

In our book Profitable Social Media Marketing, we use the example of the Stop Online Piracy Act which was a US bill to attempt to combat online copyright infringement. The act was hugely unpopular online and it quickly became apparent that the bill was not going to pass. Numerous websites and individuals decided to champion the 'Stop SOPA' cause, thus aligning themselves with the public against an enemy that was very unlikely to fight back.

If you don't like fighting, pick a defenseless enemy.

Outreach to Authority Figures

Every market has authority figures. These high profile people have influence over the market through their endorsements, and you can tap into this influence by forging associations with them.

These associations don't have to be official. Even exchanging a few tweets can give your business implied endorsement from these authority figures, increase your visibility with their audience and boost your follower count. But how do you go about attracting their attention?

Just like customers, the question that is going through their heads is 'What's in it for me?' Any time that you want to attract endorsement, you need to make sure that their needs are being met. Simply asking for a Retweet or share is unlikely to result in the sort of exposure you really want. Instead, consider asking them for an interview about their opinion on future trends in your industry, comment on something specific, or get their tips for success. The interview can be conducted by email and you can simply upload it to your blog. Your interviewee will be inclined to share the link as it helps to boost their own profile and credibility, and you'll enjoy a credibility boost from being the interviewer.

Make sure that the page containing the interview has prominent social media links to make it easy for people to follow and like you. You might also want to run a targeted offer or lead generation campaign around the interview to make the most of the traffic coming to the site.

If you can't get an interview with your authority figures, consider asking their opinions on industry news. If your questions are intelligent and allow them to demonstrate their knowledge, you can get on their radar and work yourself in over time.

Use Social Media searching to find potential customers

If your business solves a particular need, Twitter's search feature can be a great way to find potential customers. By searching for uses of certain words or phrases that represent the problem or need you are solving, you can find people tweeting about that exact problem. If you're a local business you can target particular areas to make sure that your outreach isn't wasted on those outside your catchment.

The best way to understand this is through examples:

Let's say that Mick Johnson of MJ Photography wants to book his wedding photographers some more wedding shoots across Northern Ireland. He's also identified that they're not too busy during the week, so he'd like to start offering engagement photo shoots to give his togs something to do Monday-Friday. He decides to make his Twitter profile a bit more presentable, include benefit statements and make sure it's 100% clear that his company offers excellent engagement and wedding photography shoots in Northern Ireland. He then heads over to http://nearbytweets.com, enters Northern Ireland in the location box and 'engaged' as his keyword. Up pops a list of recent tweets in Northern Ireland containing the word engaged, some of which are delighted women soon to be married.

Mick can send a congratulations tweet to each of the women (and men) he finds. He doesn't want it to look automated or too 'copy and paste' so he can comment on the ring, picture, area, choice of venue... anything that he can to personalise his congratulations. The tweets he sends aren't 'pitchy' or trying to sell his photography service, but because it's so rare to be sent a personal congratulation from someone you don't know on Twitter, you can be sure that each of his targets will be visiting his profile and probably his website.

It's a very simple strategy, but nevertheless there is plenty of opportunity for it to go wrong.

The first way that Mick can mess this up is by doing all of his outreach in one go. If his targets see dozens of outbound messages on his twitter feed, all within minutes of each other and all with very similar text, all of a sudden Mick has turned from being a nice guy into a spammer, and this makes his targets less likely to respond. Mick could also pitch his service in his tweets, immediately showing his hand and greatly reducing the chance that his target will visit his website. Her guard goes up immediately and she views Mick's communication as an advert rather than a personal message.

The final way Mick can get this wrong is by leaving it too long before congratulating tweeters. Performing these searches (or setting up a search pane in Tweetdeck) doesn't take long, but the benefit is that you're right there when the prospect is in heat. By making it someone's task (or yours) to run these searches every 2-3 days - or more often if the volume warrants it - you'll make sure that you're in the minds of your audience right when they're thinking about what it is that you offer.

This is what we call Outbound Social Lead Generation, and the strategy works for most types of B2C business from photographers to plumbers. What sort of tweets are your potential customers posting, and how can you identify a suitable target? The keyword research and understanding your customers' language exercises covered in the Online Marketing and SEO sections should have given you some ideas which you can test out.

Nip any potential customer service issues in the bud

The beauty of social media is the openness and visibility of communications. Potential customers are reassured if they see you responding to customer service queries in a timely and effective manner.

The downside is that failing to resolve any customer service issues is equally as visible and can turn into a bit of a nightmare. So to save you from potential problems, here is the official Exposure Ninja guide to customer service on social media:

- The more customers you serve, the more complaints you will get. No business doing decent volume is going to be 100% complaint-free, so having a policy for complaints is crucial. Expect the best, be prepared for the worst.
- Many complainers just want to be heard. Never fight a complaint or try to prove someone wrong, as you won't win them over. Instead, acknowledge their feelings ("I'm sorry you feel that way" or "I'm sorry to hear you've been having trouble with X"), and solve the problem with as little fuss as possible.

- Don't accept responsibility too readily. If there's been a widespread problem (your website has gone down or orders delayed) then by all means update people on the situation, but often taking full responsibility in public is not necessary. Saying that you'll need to look into the situation is usually much more desirable.
- The public nature of complaints over social media is what gives complainers their power. Once you've acknowledged their feelings, take the complaint private by asking them to email you an order reference, customer account number or something that allows you to investigate further. This will often diffuse the complaint as the customer feels they've been heard and they can't actually be bothered to proceed. For those who want to continue with the complaint, it means you can take the issue out of the public eye.
- Make sure to do everything you can to resolve complaints and fix the issue. Public complainers will also publicly praise companies that do a good job, so this is your chance for some corrective social media coverage
- Introduce yourself personally when dealing with complaints. It's easy to bash a faceless company on social media, but once customers become familiar with a particular person *in* the company, they tend to tone down the tirade.

Done properly, customer service over social media is a really effective sales tool because it gives your business a personality. Timely, calm and helpful responses make sure this personality is attractive to potential customers.

Understanding Facebook's edge weighting to boost visibility

Facebook's content is made of nodes and edges. Nodes are 'things': people, companies, buildings, events, associations and so on. Edges are the 'verbs' - they're interactions, likes, shares, posts, relationships and breakups.

With the vast amount of nodes and edges in your network then, how does Facebook decide which posts to show in your News Feed? Have you noticed how the same people come up over and over again? Perhaps you've found that visiting an old friend's page increases the volume of their posts showing up in your Feed?

If so, you are experiencing Facebook's Edge Weighting algorithm. Previously called Edgerank, this algorithm looks at as many as 100,000 different weighting factors to decide which posts to show on your News Feed, and in which order. But manipulating all 100,000 weighting factors for fun and profit is a time consuming task, so let's focus on the 3 main categories:

- Edge Weight. Not all edges are created equal. A 'like' is less significant than an engagement or a marriage, for example. Photos are more heavily weighted than status updates or shares. You'll notice that savvy social media users have realised that if they include a photo with their status updates, these updates seem to get more visibility. This is no accident, and it works like clockwork.

- Affinity. Edges involving people who you interact with most frequently are considered to be more interesting so they tend to be more heavily weighted. Conversely, posts by people who are of absolutely no interest to you are less likely to show up. The lesson for marketing on Facebook is to tune your posts to get engagement, whether that's likes, shares, comments or clicks through to a website. By creating engaging posts, your content is more likely to be seen. Bore people and your content will slowly begin to disappear...

- Decay. The time element of Facebook is important, but it's only one factor. In Facebook's early days the post weighting was more like Twitter: posts showed up in strict chronological order. Edge Weight and Affinity now have more effect than they used to, but recency remains an important weighting factor. The lesson? Make sure that you're posting when your target audience is most likely to be using Facebook. If you tend to post early in the morning but your audience doesn't log on until the kids are in bed at night, by the time they check Facebook your content is already miles down the page. We'll be looking at timing your Facebook posts in the next tip.

As you can see, there are small tweaks you can make to your Facebook strategy to take advantage of these weighting factors and boost your visibility. We always recommend that clients interested in observing some really effective Facebook strategy check out Mashable's Facebook page as well as some of the 'funny and amazing' video pages, as they have all achieved Edge weighting manipulation mastery to generate huge Facebook followings.

Time Your Facebook Posts for Maximum Engagement

As mentioned in the previous tip, understanding *who* your audience is and <u>when</u> they are online can help you to take advantage of the time decay Edge weighting in Facebook to make sure that they're seeing your posts. Every audience is slightly different and each demographic has a peak usage time, so rather than strictly obeying 'rules' about the best time to post to maximise engagement, we advocate testing what works best for you. Having said that we're a fan of taking an educated first guess, so here are some useful general usage patterns to keep an eye out for:

- 80% of 18-44 year olds check their smartphone on waking*
- 86% of mobile internet users use their device while watching TV*

- The biggest spike in conversations (posts and comments) happens at 3pm on weekdays **
- Wednesday sees the most activity, whilst Sunday sees the least **

*Results taken from an IDC Study available on https://fb-public.app.box.com/s/3iq5x6uwnqtq7ki4q8wk
**Study by Virtue, as reported on Mashable: http://mashable.com/2010/10/28/facebook-activity-study/

To begin finding your own optimal posting time, the first step is to look back through your history of posts and see which generated the most interactions. Bear in mind that the timing of your posts is only one factor in the number and quality of interactions they receive, but if you have a lot of posts to study you might begin to see patterns.

If you are friends with a number of people matching your typical customer's profile, the next step is to observe when they're most active. Again this is not a scientific study, but gives us a good base to test from. You're not only looking for times of the day, but also days of the week.

By now you should have some ideas about your audience's patterns, so it's time to test. As you continue to post, try combining your schedule with posts that are designed to get more interaction and refine this strategy over time.

What do the fastest-growing social media accounts have in common? Without exception, they all provide some sort of value to their audience, whether it's entertainment, motivation or instruction. On the other hand, what do most business social media accounts have in common? Yep, you guessed it. A complete *lack* of value to the audience.

An effective way to structure all of your marketing is to think how you can move your audience closer to their goals. This focus keeps you relevant and interesting to them, rather than a nuisance peppering their feed with adverts. Identifying how you can help your audience starts by understanding their core need that your product or service addresses.

Some examples:
- A car mechanics helps her audience enjoy trouble-free use of their car. All her marketing communications can be geared around helping her audience get closer to this goal. Seasonal recommendations, troubleshooting tips, signs that your car might need some work... All of these would make good social media topics and help grow the business's audience.
- A nursery school helps parents raise happy, sociable, well-educated children. With that as their goal, they might decide to use their social

media channels to share suggested weekend activities, studies, recommendations on further reading, nutrition tips and anything else that might help a parent raise even a 1% smarter, happier well-adjusted child. This sort of content would be far more effective at attracting a large qualified social media audience than the typical social media dross.

- Exposure Ninja helps businesses attract more customers from the Internet. With that as our goal, our social media communication tends to focus on Google updates, tips, tricks and strategies and anything else that will help businesses get more customers from the Internet.

Notice how well your competitors are doing this. Are their Newsfeeds full of self promotion and boring communication, or are they actively trying to help their audience get closer to their goals?

Choose your Facebook profile and cover images to increase conversions

If you're active on Facebook, your page will form the first impression for a significant number of potential customers. Remember that it's still a landing page, and the rules of first impressions still apply. This makes your cover photo is one of the most important and visible elements on your page.

Some approaches to the cover photo that work well:

- Using the cover photo to promote a lead generation offer.
- Use your cover photo to illustrate or explain what differentiates you from your competitors.
- Use your cover photo to add personality to your business if it's relevant.
- Demonstrate the key benefit or solution that you're offering in a way that is easily recognisable to your audience.
- Seek to eliminate the main block or objection that your audience faces which stops them from making a purchase.

Your profile picture is like an advert for your page that's visible across Facebook. Many brands will choose to use their logo as their profile picture, and this is a good approach if you're trying to build brand recognition and your audience is already familiar with you. Another approach that can work well is to concisely display your key benefit in your profile picture, or show your target audience something that will immediately grab their interest.

One of our clients is a car tuning service, and for this sort of business it made sense not to use their logo (they had very low brand recognition amongst their target audience) but instead to use a picture of a car typical of the sort that their customers owned (or aspired to own). When someone shared a status or liked their page, friends matching the target audience can immediately identify with the business and it resonates instantly. It matches what they're interested in, so it's more likely to get a click. On the other hand, a picture of their logo would not have triggered any recognition, so would be less likely to attract a click.

Lastly, if you do choose to use your logo as your profile picture and you happen to have a very wide logo, you'll need to get a square version made for social media profiles. An empty white box with a skinny, barely visible logo right in the centre won't do you any favours and gives a very poor first impression.

Integrate Social Media on your website to boost conversions

We are big fans of integrating social media with your website for three main reasons:
1. It can boost conversion
2. It can grow your following
3. It's good from an SEO point of view

To back up a little before we dive in, by 'integrating' we mean showing a Twitter and/or Facebook feed on the site connected to your business profile. Integrated social media is <u>not</u> simply having a 'Tweet This' or 'Share This' button on each of your blog posts.

The beauty of integrated social feeds on your website is that they immediately show visitors just how 'alive' you are. In the Website section we looked at the issue of building trust amongst visitors, and active Twitter and

Facebook pages tell visitors: here we are, we're popular and we're here should anything go wrong. That sense of accountability and presence is not easy to otherwise replicate online which is why if you're running social accounts they should be visible on your site, and not just through links to the profile pages.

Twitter and Facebook provide pre made widgets which you can add to your site by copying and pasting the code. If you're using Wordpress there are also a number of plugins which display feeds in widget areas on your site and they offer perhaps the simplest way to get started with minimal technical involvement.

However you choose to do it, make sure that your feeds include a Follow or Like button so that people can join your audience with one click.

Optimise the balance between sales pitches and information

To keep your audience interested on social media, you need to find the right balance between pitching and preaching. Businesses who do nothing but pitch their services numb their audience and lose listeners, whilst those who never pitch are wasting an opportunity to sell and are, frankly, being too soft.

We don't believe there's a magic ratio (some experts recommend 5 times as much 'content' as sales message) because when done properly, the sales pitch can be disguised as content. In order to strike a good balance, imagine that your social media followers were paying to receive your updates. This will help you to respect their attention. Besides, time is money so really they *are* paying to receive your updates!

What sort of information should you include in your posts?

- Latest news, and your interpretation of it. This should be posted on your blog then linked in your social media profiles, including a picture.
- Interesting articles from other websites in your market.
- Questions and surveys to your audience.
- Entertainment/personality stuff that gives your audience a glimpse into the business (but remember to keep it positive whenever possible. Nobody wants to read about or associate with ongoing struggle unless there's a happy ending).

Over time you'll find your own balance between sales and pure value messages. Remember that your audience has plenty of options online, and if you bore them or abuse the trust they put in you to provide them with value, you'll lose them.

Paid Advertising and Google Adwords

We are big fans of paid advertising, and we've been lucky enough to play a part in some amazing business launches and turnarounds thanks to the power of well-run paid ad campaigns. In this section we'll go through some general paid ad tips and take a look at social media paid advertising opportunities. At the end, we'll finish up with a short Google Adwords Pay Per Click course, which takes you step-by-step through the process of setting up and optimising a Google Adwords campaign.

Remember that as a reader of this book you can claim your Free 7-point Online Marketing Review, which includes a thorough Pay Per Click review. If you'd like to take advantage of this, go to www.exposureninja.com/101

Put your best foot forward in Ad copy

If you Google your target keyphrase, the chances are high that you'll see plenty of adverts. And the chances remain high that most of these ads will all be very similar.

Because most business owners aren't professional advertisers, writing adverts is not a part of their daily life. They come to the (logical) conclusion that in order to get a headstart, the best option is to copy the competitors' ads and try to improve on them slightly to attract more clicks. While there are certainly things to learn from your competitors' ads, there is another approach that tends to bring a higher return than 'me too' advertising.

The first step in crafting a compelling ad is to list the things that are most important about your business to your customers, and keep going until you've completely run out. Perhaps it's free shipping, low prices, high quality materials or extremely limited quantities available. Maybe the biggest draw to your business is the lead generation bait that you offer (if so, that's a sign that you've got some very compelling lead generation bait).

Whatever the hooks that attract customers to you are, they should be the things you use in your adverts. Don't shy away from being specific about how much you charge if all your competitors are hide behind 'Get a Quote', for example. Be proud of anything that makes you different, and anything that positions you against everybody else in your market only makes you more visible.

This goes for all marketing, but is really clear in Adwords where businesses enter a 4 line shoot out against each other.

Imagine your customer faced with a choice of 10 identical businesses. Being 'me too' gives you an average 1 in 10 chance of getting the gig. But if you take yourself out of that group and instead face them head to head, your customer now has *two* options - you or one of the 9 clones. This has just significantly improved your odds.

Use Facebook Advertising to Laser Target Your Audience

Facebook offers a lot of opportunities to target different groups of people, and their new retargeting feature is particularly exciting.

Before we dive into the specifics, let's take a look at why Facebook is such an important ad platform.

Target people by likes and interests

There's a fundamental difference between advertising on Facebook and advertising with Google Adwords, and that is the type of traffic you are targeting. With Adwords your ad is appearing in front of people who have expressed a particular need by searching. With Facebook you can target people by their characteristics, likes and interests. While some businesses naturally suit need-based targeting (for example a plumber: when you need them you need them, and when you don't, you don't), others suit this characteristic-based targeting because their offering doesn't necessarily meet a pressing need. An example might be a weight loss product, musician or local restaurant that wants to target a particular demographic and convert their target without them ever expressing a need.

Be visible where your competitors aren't

Another advantage of Facebook advertising is that your ad will usually be the only ad offering your particular product or service on the page. Very few businesses have explored Facebook advertising to anything like its full extent, so if you can put together an attractive offer that converts well, you'll have no direct advertising competitors.

Potentially very high ROI

While the ROI obviously depends as much on your offer and audience as it does the media, because Facebook in general attracts fewer advertisers, competition is lower and ad prices are very attractive.

Facebook uses CTR (Click Through Rate, or the percentage of your audience that clicks your ad) as a factor in determining your cost per click, so by offering a really attractive offer (generating a high CTR) it's possible to get the advert cost extremely low.

Set up your first Facebook Ad campaign

To start your first campaign, resist the pull of your timeline and head to https://www.facebook.com/advertising and click the Create an Ad button.

You'll see an option to choose the type of ad you want to run according to your goal. A word of caution here:

many businesses opt straight for the Page Likes target, assuming that the whole point of Facebook advertising is to generate more likes and engagement with their page. However, page likes is a bit of a vanity statistic and has little effect on the profitability of an ad campaign. Since we're focused primarily on your profit, we'll be taking a dive into attracting clicks to your website.

As with any advertising campaign, the first step is to plan a specific offer that you can use to elicit a direct response from your audience. This offer could be your lead generation campaign, a free trial, money off voucher or anything else that has perceived value in excess of the effort required to claim it. Our dental clients have success offering discounted checkups or teeth whitening services for example, because these are good at getting new patients through the door in order to build a relationship and sell additional treatments.

You'll need a page on your website which talks about this offer, provides enough information about you and positions your business so that new visitors feel comfortable claiming whatever it is that you're offering. This will be the landing page that you'll send people to so that they can claim your offer.

In Facebook choose the Clicks to your Website option and put in the URL of this landing page. Many new advertisers make the mistake of directing traffic straight to their homepage, which is less than ideal because it's non targeted and often not particularly relevant to the goal your prospect had in mind when they clicked.

Once you've put in your landing page URL, you'll see Facebook grab some pictures that you might want to use in your ad. Remember that the pictures you use are more important than even the headline, so you want something that is going to stand out in your audience's newsfeed and, if possible, demonstrates the benefit of your product or service. By uploading different pictures, you can test the relative responses to each and find out which works most effectively for you.

When creating a headline and description for your ad, remember to answer the question on repeat in your audience's mind: "what's in it for me?" Mention the benefits of what you offer rather than talking too much about your business itself, and use any tantalising details to attract curiosity and persuade them to click on the ad and visit your landing page. You're unlikely to make a sale from the ad alone, so the most you can hope is to attract qualified potential customers and intrigue them enough to be receptive to the message on your landing page.

In the Advanced Options section you can enter the News Feed description for your link. This is really important because it appears underneath the image like a caption and attracts a lot of eyeballs. Make sure that this description positions your business as highly relevant and specialist to the product or service that you are promoting.

Targeting your Audience

You'll want to narrow the target audience of your ad, and you have the options to target them according to geography, age, gender, interests, relationship status and preference, language, education and workplaces. As you narrow your focus you'll see the Estimated Audience number adjust to reflect the number of Facebook users in the middle of your increasingly complex Venn diagram.

Choosing Pricing

You'll need to set a daily or total budget at which point your ads will stop showing. As for the bidding on ad costs, there are 2 options: Optimise for Clicks or Impressions. If the goal of your ad is to get people on your website, filling in forms or buying, then choose optimise for clicks. If you're running a 'branding' or 'awareness' campaign, then optimising for impressions will give you the most views of your ad.

Once you're ready to begin, click Place Order. Your advert will be reviewed by someone from Facebook before going live.

Targeting Website Conversions in Facebook Ads

If you like the sound of Facebook advertising and want to get a little bit more advanced, they offer a feature called Website Conversions. This allows you to measure actions that people take on your website through the Facebook advertising platform so that you can optimise your ad campaign to target conversions. To do this, you'll need to create a tracking pixel and place this on your site. Follow the instructions to create your pixel, and add the tracking code to the page displayed when somebody has converted. For example if you want to track form completions (get a quote or contact us), make sure to install the code on the Thankyou page. If you want to track an e-commerce sale, install the code on the Checkout Complete page.

Once you've created and installed your tracking pixel it can take a while for it to be verified by Facebook. In the meantime, you can head back to the advertising setup page to start creating your Website Conversions campaign. The advert creation is the same process as in the previous tip, but because the whole campaign is focussed on attracting the most conversions for your budget, the bid optimisation is by default configured around website conversions. You can choose to optimise for Clicks or Impressions instead by opening the Advanced Pricing section.

Create and Promote Facebook Offers

As big fans of specific and measurable offers, the promotion of offers through Facebook advertising is the sort of thing that we Ninjas get really excited about. Offers are great because they can be really simple to understand. A free trial, discount on a product, consultation or bonus is something with clear value that doesn't require too much explanation and can be a really effective hook to get your audience's attention. When claiming an offer, new customers receive an email that they can present to you in order to claim the discount. If they can claim the offer online then you can activate a discount code system, or simply give everybody access.

To begin go to www.facebook.com/ads/create and choose Offer Claims. Choose your business's page to see any eligible offers that you have already created or click on the + button to create a new one.

As always, make sure that your offer description qualifies your target audience, demonstrates relevance and clearly states the benefits of what you're offering. You don't have much space, so best not to waste too much room giving specifics about the offer aside from the necessary basics. Choose an image that catches the eye and reflects the benefit in your offer.

In the redemption details screen you can add an offer expiration date as well as any terms and conditions. The advanced options allow you to set a redemption link if your offer is available online. If you'd like to create a QR code, barcode or online promo code, you can enter the code details that the customer will be given. Obviously if you're setting an online promo code to give a discount on your website, you'll need to set up the voucher code element on your site as well. If you need any help with this, do get in touch and we'll be happy to advise.

One final handy trick: if you want to advertise your offer on people's newsfeeds but don't necessarily want to promote it on your *page's* feed, you can click the crosshair icon at the bottom of the Offer post. This is useful if you want to advertise the offer only to a specific target audience without giving away too much to your wider (or existing) audience.

ADWORDS PAY PER CLICK CRASH COURSE

Adwords is one of the most important and potentially profitable marketing channels online, and there are very few businesses (we haven't found any yet in over 300) who can't make money from a well-run Adwords campaign.

At the same time, we're also yet to find an Adwords advertiser who can't implement some tweaks to their campaign to cut costs further whilst wringing out some extra profit. The difference to your bottom line between having a basic understanding of Adwords and really mastering it can be significant.

Over the course of the remaining tips, we'll go through the Adwords Pay Per Click Crash Course, designed to help new advertisers get started, and existing advertisers squeeze out some extra profit from their campaigns.

Understand and Maximise Ad Rank to increase your ad positioning

Just like Google's organic search results use an algorithm to determine ranking, Adwords uses its own ranking algorithm to decide the position of each advert. This algorithm is called Ad Rank and comprises of a few different elements:

- Your CPC (Cost Per Click) bid. This is how much you are willing to pay for each click on your ad. Generally a higher CPC bid leads to higher Ad Rank, and resulting higher position.

- Quality Score. This is a combination of the quality and relevance of your ads, their CTR (Click Through Rate, or percentage of visitors that click on the ad) and the content of your website. Yes, your website affects the cost of your advertising. Remember that Google only wants to show the highest quality and most relevant websites, even if they're paying for the privilege, so a well-optimised landing page will mean your ad tends to rank higher for the same cost.
- Use of Ad Extensions. Extensions are 'add ons' that you can include with your ad. Examples are links to different pages on your site, phone numbers, Google+ links and physical address information. Not only do these Ad Extensions give your ad more space on the page, but they are also taken into consideration by the Ad Rank algorithm to reward advertisers that use them.

Ad Rank is calculated every time your advert is eligible to appear, so you are essentially entering into an auction with the other advertisers each time somebody searches for your target phrase.

One of the most misunderstood elements of Adwords is the Quality Score component. Many advertisers wanting to position their ad higher on the page will simply set a higher CPC bid, neglecting to improve their adverts, optimise their campaign or improve the relevance of the website itself. This approach is the equivalent of the parent who doesn't have time to spend with their child, so they resort to buying expensive gifts. It gets very expensive and the result is still not as effective. Plus, in the case of Adwords, the child is Google. And if there's *anyone* who doesn't need any more of your money, it's Google. So rather than reaching for the credit card to feed it more money, work on improving the quality of your advert and website to boost quality score.

Organise your campaign structure for maximum profit

The organisation and structure of your Adwords campaign is key to its profitability. Maximising the ROI of Adwords is about removing lots of small inefficiencies and finely tuning and optimising every detail. For that reason, it's important to get everything in order early on, before we get down to making any tweaks and changes. A properly organised Adwords account gives you greater control and allows clearer monitoring of each ad group, keyword and campaign.

Campaigns

Campaigns are the top level of your Adwords advertising. We recommend setting up a separate Campaign for each main product or service in order to be able to allocate budget and clearly monitor results on a per-product or per-service basis:

- Campaign (Main product or service)

- Ad Group (Targeting a particular search for this product or service)
- Ad Group (Targeting a variation of the search for this product or service)
  - Ad (An ad written to target the variation)
  - Ad (Another ad targeting the variation, but worded slightly differently to test responses)
  - Ad (Another ad written slightly differently for testing)
    - Keywords
    - Keywords
    - Keywords

If we take an example of a lettings/rental company, they might be running ads to find tenants for 1 bedroom, 2 bedroom and 3 bedroom apartments. Their competitors might bundle all of these together and simply run a 'Rentals' ad campaign, but this would result in huge wastage and prevent proper segmentation. It would also reduce the overall Quality score of the ads, resulting in higher costs per click.

So the optimal Adwords structure would look like:
- Campaign: 1 Bedroom Apartments
- Campaign: 2 Bedroom Apartments
- Campaign: 3 Bedroom Apartments

It's this level of segregation that allows us to remove wastage and optimise each campaign to boost quality score and reduce the CPC of each ad.

Ad Groups

Once you have each product or service as a separate Campaign, the next step is breaking it down further into Ad Groups. Ad Groups hold different variations of grammar ("one" vs "1", for example), niches ("pets" or "smokers") and keyword modifiers ("cheap", for example).

The best way to illustrate this is to continue with the example. Inside the *1 Bedroom Apartments* campaign, we would have a series of Ad Groups targeted to the possible variations:

- Campaign: 1 Bedroom Apartments
  - Ad Group: 1 Bedroom Apartments
  - Ad Group: Cheap 1 Bedroom Apartments
  - Ad Group: One Bedroom Apartments
  - Ad Group: Pets 1 Bedroom

You'll notice that each of these Ad Groups is relevant to the '1 Bedroom Apartments' Campaign. To add a 2 Bedroom Apartments Ad Group, you would have to add a new Campaign targeting 2 Bedroom Apartments, as Groups should not cover more than one product or service. This keeps the Campaign clean, tidy and makes sure that every Ad Group relates to the subject of the Campaign. This is what Google wants to see, and rewards with higher Quality Scores.

With such precisely targeted Ad Groups, we can now move onto creating the Ads themselves.

Writing effective Adwords ads

Our magic formula for writing effective ads is as follows:

Title goes here
Key benefit statement
Call to action
www.domain.com/keyword

A killer title

The best ad titles include the target keywords. Remember that this is the phrases the searcher has typed in, so it's the phrase that their eyes are scanning for and that Google will be highlighting in bold.

First Line

The first line of your text should include a key benefit: a reason why the searcher should click on this ad and choose you over your competitors. Some effective benefit statements include specific prices (if you are competitive on price), additional features or special offers (the more specific and tantalising, the better).

Second Line

Your second line should be a clear call to action explaining exactly what you want the searcher to do. If you have space for a final benefit or USP, then this is a good place to include it. This could be "Free delivery - order today", "Call to book now - 20% off" (in conjunction with a phone number ad extension).

Display URL

The display URL is one that you choose yourself. The domain must match the domain of the target site, and you should include your target keyword afterwards to boost the relevance of your ad further.

Let's look at a complete ad for the Rental example:

1 Bedroom Apartments
From $699 - With Car Park
Book Today - Call or Email
Ninjaproperty.com/1-Bedroom

As you can see, the title matches the keyword, the first line contains key benefit statements (starting price and car park), and the second line contains a clear CTA and instructions to book an appointment. This type of ad would typically run with a phone number extension as well, meaning that interested parties could call straight from the ad without having to visit the site. Finally, the display URL contains the name of the site and the keyword.

You'll notice that the ad relates to a 1 bedroom apartment, as does the Ad Group and the Campaign. By keeping all of these strictly related, you'll typically see a decrease in CPC of around 10%. This strategy alone has saved some of our clients upwards of £50,000.

Keyword selection secrets of the pros

The most profitable PPC campaigns not only focus on which keywords to target, but also specify those to *exclude*. Typically, when we analyse a client's Adwords campaign we find that they're wasting approximately

20% of their budget on unwanted clicks as a result of showing up for searches that they have absolutely no relevance to. Just by looking through the past trigger searches and excluding any clearly irrelevant search terms, we are typically able to save a client our entire fee for the duration of the campaign.

To illustrate what makes a good keyword list, let's continue with the rental example:

In the Ad Group 1 Bedroom Apartments, with our ad titled 1 Bedroom Apartments, our keywords might be:

- 1 bedroom apartments (Type: Exact match)
- 1 bedroom apartment (Type: Exact match)
- +1 +bedroom +apartments (Type: Broad match)
- +1 +bedroom +apartment (Type: Broad match)

The first two keywords are exact match, which means that the ad will be triggered if the searcher uses the terms **exactly** as we've entered them. You'll notice we've included both the singular and plural for apartments.

The final two keywords are modified broad match. Broad match means that the ad shows whenever a term is used, no matter what the order. Unmodified broad match would mean that variations or similar words would also trigger our ad, but because in this case we've added the '+' modifier, each term is required before the ad will show. The result of this targeting is that the ad will show when someone searches for any arrangement of the words, or with additional words included

An example of this could be a user searching for:

nice 1 bedroom apartments 🔍

This would trigger our advert because it has matched the broad keywords '1', 'bedroom' and 'apartments'.

Another valid example would be if a user was searching for:

1 bedroom apartments london ontario 🔍

Again this would trigger our Ad because all three broad keywords have been searched.

So what type of search *wouldn't* trigger our ad?

2 bedroom apartments london ontario 🔍

This search term would not trigger our Ad because not all three broad keywords were matched.

Adding Negative Keywords

Choosing negative keywords for your campaign is like writing the guest list for your birthday party. Some keywords might create unwanted impressions and clicks (unpleasant moments) that you would prefer to avoid, and certainly avoid paying for.

Negative keywords are like a 'no entry' list for your ads. Any time one of these words shows up, your ad isn't shown. Using negative keywords can say you a lot of money and make sure that your ads are only showing for those who are qualified to buy from you, increasing your ROI.

The sort of keywords you might want to block are those that indicate the searcher does not match your selection criteria. They might be unable to buy from you, unwilling or you might have identified that people making this search are still in the research phase, thus not worth your Adwords spend.

Let's imagine Ninja Cakes, a luxury custom cake shop run by ninjas. Their target audience is those getting married or buying expensive customised birthday or special occasion cakes. In their luxury birthday cakes campaign, they decide to target the phrase "luxury birthday cakes", and want to add some negative keywords to increase their ROI.

Some search terms they might want to exclude with negative keywords could be:

- "Cheap" - indicating that the searcher does not have the budget for a fine ninja cake.
- "Recipe" - indicating the searcher is looking to make their own cake rather than buy one.
- "Asda"/"Walmart"/"Tesco" - the presence of supermarket chains in the search terms would again suggest a lower budget than is required, or significantly different buying habits.
- "Classes"/"Class" - unlike us, these cake making ninjas don't share their secrets, so they don't offer classes and therefore don't want to pay to advertise to those who are looking to learn how to make luxury cakes.

Remember that increasing ROI in Adwords is often about removing lots of small inefficiencies to focus your advertising on high quality traffic only. By adding these negative keywords to their Campaigns, Ninja Cakes can save their ad budget from being used to attract unsuitable visitors, leaving more budget to target these suitable visitors.

Choose your target audience carefully

You can choose the locations that your ads will target, either by name or by radius from a particular location. This needs very little explanation other than to make sure that you do it. It's very frustrating to see local companies who haven't set their location targeting correctly appearing in searches halfway across the country for people who are totally unable to buy from them. It hurts Click Through Rate as people don't click on the ad if it's obviously targeted outside their area, and lower click through rates mean lower Quality Score, and consequently demand a higher Cost Per Click.

Location targeting is done at the Campaign level, so if you want to location target your ads you'll need to set up a separate campaign for each product or service in each location. If you're thinking that it sounds like a lot of effort, you're right. And it's exactly why your competitors won't do it... and how we're able to reduce costs per click by as much as 50% for some clients.

Use Automated Rules to stay above your competitors

Automated rules in Adwords keep an eye on your competitors while you work, rest or play. Think of them as your own Adwords assistant working 24 hours a day, 7 days a week carrying out your instructions. Given the right instructions, they can be a really useful ally.

Unsurprisingly, the top three ad positions (those shown on the left hand side of the page) outperform those on the right hand side, so many advertisers like to make sure their ads are always in this prominent position. To do this without setting a consistently high Maximum Cost Per Click, you can set up an Automated Rule that increases your CPC bid by a certain amount (we tend to use 5-10%) when your average ad position falls below 3. It's important to monitor this type of rule to begin with, and we always recommend setting an upper limit for CPC to prevent billing 'surprises'!

You can also use Automated rules to schedule ads for special promotions, turn ads on or off during specific periods (for example to run a different set of ads at weekends), pause low performing keywords or ads (to prevent Quality Score losses) and pause campaigns that meet a daily budget.

To get started with Automated rules, click Automate from inside your Adwords account. You'll be able to choose from a list of triggers, and specify what should happen when the trigger fires.

You can set the frequency of your rules to define how often they should run, and the results are collected in a log. These logged results allow you to monitor the effects of your rules to ensure that they are having the desired effect. Things can get out of hand quite quickly if rules aren't monitored and stops aren't put in place to prevent budgets steadily increasing, for example.

Exploit Remarketing

Remarketing has made a lot of advertisers rich, and is one of the most significant innovations in the history of advertising. Remarketing allows you to target visitors to your website, after they've left and while they're surfing the rest of the Internet. If you've noticed how ads for some E-commerce sites seem to follow you around, showing you products that you viewed but didn't purchase, you've seen remarketing in action. It works and, if properly set up, it's ridiculously profitable.

By placing a tracking pixel on your website, Google can install a cookie on your site visitors' computers. If you have remarketing configured, and provided that this user has met your remarketing criteria, each time they visit a website in Google's Display Network, they'll see a remarketing ad for your website. This can be a good opportunity to remind them about you, for example by offering them an additional incentive to come back and buy from you.

The beauty of remarketing is the complicated set up. This complexity is so beautiful because it discourages most businesses from getting started, even though they know it could potentially make a big difference to their business.

What sort of businesses stand to benefit most from remarketing?

If your business involves a pre-sale research phase, this is the ideal time to begin remarketing. When your potential customers are researching their buying options, they are at the most impressionable. They're also learning a lot which means that sometimes your site, products or services can be forgotten.

E-commerce sites fall into this category and cart-abandonments are a logical event to target because they signal buyer intent, but fall short of making the sale. Service businesses also make good candidates for profitable remarketing campaigns as there is usually a period of research and comparison before a provider is chosen. If you can increase your visibility through remarketing, you'll be 'front of mind' while the prospect is making their decision.

With the recent announcement from Facebook that they are rolling their own remarketing service out, allowing website owners to remarket their websites to visitors on Facebook, 2014 is going to be the year that remarketing really comes of age.

If you need any help implementing remarketing, just drop us a line through the Exposure Ninja website and we'll be more than happy to help.

What next?

So there you have it: 101 tips plus a few extras that we really wanted to include. What you do next will determine the value you get from this book, and whether it will have a significant effect on your business or not.

The next step is to head over to www.exposureninja.com/101, if you haven't already, as you'll be able to claim some free goodies to get you started on your journey.

One of these goodies is the most valuable gift in Internet Marketing. The FREE 7 Point Online Marketing Review from our world-class experts comes complete with a strategic plan to attract more business from your website. This analysis is worth £186 + VAT, but we're offering it free to readers of this book to give you an extra helping hand.

The nature of Tips books is that each tip is given, at most, a few pages. The truth is that some of the tips in this book could easily form the basis of an entire chapter or video course, and while we've sought to give you an easily digestible overview, you might find it useful to dig a little deeper.

We are here to help, and are happy to offer advice through our website, email or over the phone. Our team of Internet Marketing ninjas are the sharpest in the business, and we love nothing more than getting a big fat juicy testimonial from a client we've saved or made a lot of money for.

If you enjoyed this book, I'd really appreciate a review on Amazon. It makes a big difference, and we enjoy reading them.

If you have any feedback, you can contact me personally by email: tim@exposureninja.com

Printed in Great Britain
by Amazon.co.uk, Ltd.,
Marston Gate.